POLITICS AND REVIEWERS: THE *EDINBURGH* AND THE *QUARTERLY*

in the early Victorian age

JOANNE SHATTOCK

Leicester University Press
(a division of Pinter Publishers Ltd)
London, Leicester and New York

PN
5130
E35
S5
1989

© Joanne Shattock 1989

First published in 1989 by Leicester University Press
(a division of Pinter Publishers Limited)

Tallahassee, Florida

Editorial Offices
Fielding Johnson Building, University of Leicester
University Road, Leicester, LE1 7RH

Trade and other enquiries
25 Floral Street, London, WC2E 9DS

British Library Cataloguing in Publication Data
A CIP cataloguing record for this book is available
from the British Library
ISBN 0-7185-1269-3

Library of Congress Cataloging-in-Publication Data
CIP Data available from the Library of Congress

Printed in Great Britain by
Billing & Sons Ltd, Worcester

CONTENTS

For M.L.S., F.E.S. and T.E.L.S.

PREFACE

This book has grown out of a long term interest in what might be called the phenomenon of the nineteenth century quarterly Review, the prestigious, influential, mandarin periodical form of the early to mid-century, which originated with the *Edinburgh Review*, founded in 1802, followed by the *Quarterly* in 1809. I am concerned with the impact of the quarterlies, their role in the literary and cultural world in general and their connections with the political parties and movements to which they gave allegiance, and to which, to a certain extent, they owed their foundation.

I am not, in this book, directly concerned with what the quarterlies actually said on particular issues or events, or on their response to individual writers or works. These aspects of reviewing have been dealt with extensively elsewhere and are, for the most part, well known. Rather, I am concerned to explore the actual workings of the Reviews, the recruiting of reviewers and the writing of review articles, the pressures of conducting a major literary and political organ, the creation of the delicate balance between the literary content of each issue and its political stance, and the extended rivalry of the two original Reviews. I am interested, too, in the sense that reviewers, editors and proprietors had of the status of the enterprise in which they were engaged, and of the nature of review writing as set against, on the one hand, writing for newspapers or magazines and, on the other, the writing of books.

The earliest days of the *Edinburgh* and the *Quarterly* have been dealt with by, among others, John Clive in his *Scotch Reviewers: The Edinburgh Review, 1802–1815* (1957), and in an earlier work by Hill and Helen Shine, *The Quarterly Review under Gifford* (1949). I have taken up the story with the second editorial generation, the successors to Jeffrey at the *Edinburgh* and Gifford at the *Quarterly*, which, in the first instance, coincided with a change in government, the emergence of the *Edinburgh* as a 'government' Review, as opposed to an opposition journal, and the *Quarterly*'s corresponding relegation. The 1830s, for my purposes, present an interesting period in the history of quarterly reviewing and of periodical publication generally. It was also the last decade, I believe, in which the quarterlies had a significant political influence.

I am indebted to many individuals and institutions for help both in the writing and in the research for this book. In particular, my colleagues Philip Collins, Lois Potter and Michael Slater generously took the time to read the manuscript and to make many valuable comments. Galen Williams of the manuscript department of the William L. Clements Library, University of Michigan, arranged for a new microfilm of a portion of the vast collection of J. W. Croker's Papers. Virginia Murray, of John Murray Publishers, was tireless in unearthing material relating to the *Quarterly* from the firm's extensive archives. Sue Lloyd of the Victorian Studies Centre, University of Leicester, provided invaluable assistance in the final stages. The inter-library loan department of Leicester University Library efficiently located many unlikely sources, and the Research Board of the University generously gave me two grants in aid of research.

I have also benefited from the comments and criticisms of various audiences to whom I have presented papers. I am particularly grateful to the conference on Literature and Politics at the City University of New York, 1982, the conference of the Research Society for Victorian Periodicals at the University of Toronto, 1985, the Australasian Victorian Studies Association conference at the University of New England, 1988, and to members of the seminar on Newspaper and Periodical History at the Institute for Historical Research, University of London.

Some of the material in Chapters 1 and 2 was published in an earlier form in the *Yearbook of English Studies*, X (1980), and XVI (1986).

Leicester, November 1988   *Joanne Shattock*

Chapter 1

REVIEWS, REVIEWERS AND READERS

'To be an Edinburgh Reviewer is, I suspect, the highest rank in modern literary society.' Hazlitt's comment, even allowing for a hint of irony, suggested the status and prominence which quarterly reviews had attained by their second decade of existence, a position they were to maintain until well into mid-century. The remark chimed nicely with Walter Bagehot's observation in 1855 that his generation in its youth had regarded the appearance of the *Edinburgh* as 'a grave constitutional event' and had been told that its composition was entrusted to 'Privy Councillors only'. Again, allowing for the somewhat ponderous jest, the comment was an acknowledgement by a later generation of the quarterlies' early achievement. However, Bagehot, and later Leslie Stephen and John Morley, were to look back on the great days of quarterly reviewing with more sober scrutiny and to find that achievement, in literary terms, at least, less substantial than its reputation had suggested.[1]

But to those in the midst of the fray, in the years following the founding of the *Edinburgh* in 1802 and the *Quarterly* in 1809, Hazlitt's comment would have secured general agreement. By the 1820s there was a sense of proliferation, of many Reviews springing up and of reviewing having become a dominant element of literary life. In a review of the periodical press for the *Edinburgh* in 1823, which began with the rhetorical question 'Whether periodical literature is on the whole beneficial to the cause of literature?', Hazlitt's predictable response was an emphatic 'yes', followed by the argument that the temper of the times was suited to criticism rather than creativity, that it was an age of reflection, of reconsideration and evaluation after the achievement of the immediate past. Criticism had 'never struck its roots so deep, nor spread its branches so widely and luxuriantly' as it did at the present time. The only authors not starving were periodical essayists. The only writers who kept their reputations were anonymous critics. The modern writer must give himself over to this impulse to assessment and criticism:

> Literary immortality is now let on short leases and he must be contented to succeed by rotation... we exist in the bustle of the world, and cannot escape from the notice of our contemporaries. We must please to live and therefore should live to please. We must look to the public for support... Therefore let Reviews flourish — let Magazines increase and multiply — let the Daily and Weekly newspapers live forever! We are optimists in literature, and hold, with certain limitations that, in this respect, whatever is, is right.'[2]

It was, of course, a self-serving point for one who, as Macaulay noted, was wont to say of himself, 'I am nothing if not critical.'[3]

The prevalence of Reviews and reviewing was an observable phenomenon by the 1830s. Not all of its participants, however, were as optimistic as Hazlitt. For Carlyle it was an example of literature feeding upon itself, another manifestation of modern self-consciousness which was a symptom of inner decay:

> Reviewing spreads with strange vigour; that such a man as Byron reckons the Reviewer and the Poet equal... at the last Leipzig Fair, there was advertised a Review of Reviews. By and by it will be found that all Literature has become one boundless self-devouring Review... Thus does Literature, also, like a sick thing, superabundantly 'listen to itself'.[4]

No two writers had a better grasp of the realities of professional literary life than Hazlitt and Carlyle. Both wrote extensively for Reviews, whether enthusiastically or resignedly, in the knowledge that reviewing was a livelihood and, as Hazlitt had suggested, that reviewing had become a central feature of modern literary life.

Carlyle's jaundiced vision reflected his impatience and no doubt his irritation that, until some other source of regular income was forthcoming, he was shackled to the periodical press. Posturing typically in 1835 in answer to a request from John Stuart Mill to contribute to his newly acquired *London Review*, he put the case for the reviewer faced with the necessity of earning a living and unable to commit himself to any one cause:

It were so pleasant for me, so profitable, could I, seeing clearly what I did, *unite* myself with a set of men whom I believe to have the faithfullest intentions, and take a far heartier share in their work than (as you know) writing for it now and then means with me. Alas we are fallen into wondrous times in that respect! To enter some Dog's-meat Bazaar; muffled up; perhaps holding your nose, and say: 'Here you, Master, able Editor or whatever your name is, will you buy this mess of mine (at so much per pound) and sell it among your Dog's meat?' — and then, having dealt with the able Editor, hurry out again, and wish that it could be kept secret from all men: *this* is the nature of my connection with Periodicals.[5]

But to the reviewer who could, to take up Carlyle's point, unite himself with a set of men whose common cause, however vague, he believed in, or at least did not object to, reviewing was not only a lucrative form of literary endeavour, it could also make one's reputation. Macaulay's essay on Milton, which was his second contribution to the *Edinburgh* in August 1825, set the 25-year-old contributor on a course that was to lead first to a seat in Parliament and ultimately to a career which uniquely embraced the world of politics and the world of letters.

Carlyle, Macaulay and Hazlitt were undoubtedly exceptional cases, the stars of a network which involved at one stage of their careers scientists, politicians, diplomats, civil servants, dons, clergymen, military men, novelists, poets, scholars — anyone who could answer, however tentatively or amateurishly, to the name of reviewer.

The Review was not a nineteenth-century phenomenon. The format had evolved in the mid-eighteenth century — a series of solid articles or essays, usually containing copious quotations or extracts, which attempted to describe and sometimes to appraise as many works of current literature as possible. The Reviews were conceived, as Derek Roper, their modern historian, has described them, as 'instalments of a continuous encyclopaedia, recording the advance of knowledge in every field of human enterprise'.[6] Literature in this context embraced all areas of knowledge from science and mathematics to philosophy and theology, to history and biography and literature 'proper', poetry, drama and the novel. The reviews were by definition non-specialist, their underlying assumption being that the reader was able to engage with and wished to be informed on a spectrum of subjects which in the twentieth century have become the preserve of specialists.

The original reviews — the *Monthly*, founded in 1749, the *Critical* (1756), the *English* (1783), the *Analytical* (1788) and the *British Critic* (1793) — were in part defeated by their own ambition, the determination to include as many works as possible, even to the extent of cramming what could not be reviewed into a series of short notices. But they were actually outmanœuvred, indeed virtually eclipsed when the *Edinburgh* was launched in 1802.

Henry Cockburn's impressionistic account conveyed the excitement and the impact of that event:

> The effect was electrical. And instead of expiring as many wished, in their first effort, the force of the shock was increased in each subsequent discharge. It is impossible, for those who did not live at the time, and in the heart of the scene, to feel or almost to understand, the impression made by the new luminary, or the anxieties with which its motions were observed. It was an entire and instant change of everything that the public had been accustomed to in that sort of composition.[7]

From the beginning the *Edinburgh* established precedents. It was published four times a year rather than monthly. It was determinedly free of any connections with booksellers, one of the major criticisms of the older Reviews, and it was unashamedly partisan in its politics. It was a Whig organ, just as the *Quarterly*, founded seven years later to counter its 'deleterious doctrine', was a Tory publication.[8]

By Hazlitt's account the Reviews came first and the politics second. The assessment is probably correct. So important had Reviews and reviewing become, in all areas of intellectual discussion, Hazlitt argued, that in order to make political discussion palatable, it was necessary to insert it into 'a sort of sandwich of literature'. It was a pity, he thought, that as a result, periodical criticism ran the risk of becoming the engine of party spirit and personal invective, but the natural linking of politics and literature was a testimony to the status of the Reviews, rather than to the power of political debate. The combination and the balance of the two elements, however, were to become far more problematical than the projectors of either the *Edinburgh* or the *Quarterly* could have anticipated.

The founding of the *Edinburgh* in 1802 inaugurated the era of the quarterlies, which were to become and to remain the mandarin periodical form of the nineteenth century. Authoritative, ultra-respectable and at times highly influential, they were from the outset prestigious enterprises. Archibald Constable, the first publisher of the *Edinburgh*, persuaded Francis Jeffrey, the first editor, that there should be no whiff of Grub Street in quarterly circles and that all contributors, whatever their circumstances, should be handsomely rewarded. No one, the editor included, was to be allowed to write gratuitously. Jeffrey's initial thought had been that they should be 'all gentlemen and no pay'.[9] It was this, in Walter Scott's view, which had been the single most important element in the *Edinburgh*'s initial and continuing success. In the end, John Murray, the *Quarterly*'s publisher throughout its long history, became, if anything, a more generous paymaster than either Archibald Constable or his successor Thomas Longman.

Despite their high profile, the status of the quarterlies as contrasted with the newspaper press on the one hand and the world of literature on the other, was a constant source of anxiety. In his *Life of Jeffrey*, Cockburn observed a mild schizophrenia in Jeffrey between his devotion and indeed pride in the *Edinburgh* and its Whiggish principles and his continuing fears, voiced over the years, that his connections with the Review would impede his advancement in the legal profession. Some of these worries were based on a sense that the Review's political stance would work against him, but increasingly it was the fact, as he expressed it to Cockburn in 1827, of 'being considered as fairly articled to a trade that is not perhaps the most respectable,' that might disadvantage him:

> I have been anxious to keep clear of any tradesman-like concern in the Review, and to confine myself pretty strictly to intercourse with *gentlemen* only, even as contributors. It would vex me, I must own, to find that, in spite of this, I have lowered my own character and perhaps even that of my profession, by my connection with a publication which I certainly engaged with on very Whig grounds and have managed, I think, without dirtying my hands in any paltry matters.[10]

The taint of journalism and the threat it might pose to a professional career were a constant source of worry for potential reviewers. Scott professed anxiety when his son-in-law, John Gibson

Lockhart, was offered the editorship of a newspaper which was being set up by John Murray. Lockhart himself referred emphatically to the 'loss of caste in society' that would occur if he edited a newspaper, and of the 'impossibility of my ever entering into the career of London in the capacity of a newspaper editor'. The editorship of the *Quarterly Review*, which was Murray's subsequent offer, was clearly a different matter. William Wright, a solicitor who advised Murray and who had also befriended Lockhart, made the distinction succinctly:

> Your accepting of the editorship of a newspaper would be *infra dig.*, and a losing of caste; but not so, as I think, the accepting of the editorship of the *Quarterly Review*... An editor of a Review like the *Quarterly* is the office of a scholar and a gentleman; but that of a newspaper is not, for a newspaper is merely stock-in-trade, to be used as it can be turned to most profit. And there is something in it... that is repugnant to the feelings of a gentleman...[11]

Scott used more colourful language to the same end four years later when the Duke of Wellington, through John Wilson Croker, mooted the possibility of Lockhart's assisting in yet another newspaper, this time with Treasury backing: 'Your connection with any newspaper would be a disgrace and degradation. I would rather sell gin to the poor people and poison them that way.' Lockhart needed no persuading: 'I will not, even to serve the Duke, mix myself up with newspapers. That work it is which has damned Croker.'[12]

There was no question but that the quarterlies and their contributors considered themselves quite separate from 'the Press' and its attendant evils of subservient political affiliation, paid employment and the ungentlemanly aroma of trade, or more precisely, profitmaking. Profit was something with which the proprietors of the quarterlies were not overly familiar, although they did not disregard the possibility when it presented itself. On the whole, though, they preserved a discreet silence as regards the business side of the enterprise.

The status of the quarterlies in relation to the rest of the periodical press involved subtler distinctions. The image of the magazines, as established primarily by *Blackwood's* (1817) and extended by *Fraser's* (1830), was one of at best rollicking high spirits, literary pranks and generally 'light' articles, and at worst, acerbic satire, and splenetic personal attacks. Whereas the quarterlies had *gravitas* and solidity, the magazines were measured by their entertainment value even to the point of irresponsibility. In his book *The Rise and Fall of the English Man of Letters*, John Gross compares the conduct of a quarterly to that of bringing an encyclopædia up to date, while managing a magazine, he suggests, was more like running a theatrical troupe. The analogy is a good one. One potential *Edinburgh* reviewer apologized to Macvey Napier, Jeffrey's successor, because his experience had hitherto been in writing for the monthlies, whose 'superficial nature' had not left room for the exercise of the 'graver powers'.[13] The contrast between the superficial and the grave was a popular distinction made between the magazines and the quarterlies.

Even the most confident quarterly reviewers were not entirely certain of the status of the enterprise in which they were engaged. Macvey Napier had succeeded to the *Edinburgh* in 1829 largely on the strength of his experience as editor of the *Encyclopædia Britannica*. His friend the political economist J. R. MacCulloch advised him not to relinquish his former occupation: 'It is a far higher publication than the Review, will live longer and involves one [in] less dirty political scuffles'. Hazlitt made a similar distinction when he declined Napier's invitation to write for the *Encyclopædia*, professing the inability to write with the necessary solidity: 'To get up an article in a Review on any subject of general literature is quite as much as I can do without exposing myself.'[14]

In contrast to the magazines, the quarterlies were sound, thorough and solid to the point of dullness. Compared with an encyclopaedia, they were lightweight to the point of superficiality and in danger of becoming politically tainted. The pattern was to shift as the century progressed. Dullness masquerading as solidity had been the undoing of the original Reviews, especially with their pretensions to encyclopaedic inclusiveness. Solidity was to be, ultimately, the undoing of their successors.

The *Edinburgh*, in Bagehot's words 'began the system' and became its model. In the minds of the editors and proprietors of almost every quarterly Review founded subsequently was the ambition, admitted or not, of imitating, challenging or overthrowing its position. The establishment of the *Quarterly* in 1809 was effectively the work of a breakaway group which had become dissatisfied with its politics and to a lesser extent with its style. But the *Edinburgh* was nevertheless the yardstick against which its success was constantly measured.

When the group of philosophical radicals surrounding Bentham and James Mill considered founding a quarterly Review it was to the *Edinburgh* they turned and it was significantly the *Edinburgh* that Mill chose to attack in an important article on 'Periodical Literature' in the first number of the *Westminster* (January 1824). Half a century after its foundation it was still the standard against which the *Westminster* measured its success. In 1851, long after he had relinquished any official connection with the *Westminster*, John Stuart Mill wrote to its proprietor: 'If I thought that £500 expended on the review would ... enable the *Westr* to take the place of the *Edinburgh* — I would gladly help to raise it — but I do not think there is any probability of much.'[15]

Almost from its inception the *Edinburgh* became the Review for which most reviewers wished to write and in which authors wished to be reviewed. 'I have no hesitation, for my own part, in stating what is simply a literal historical fact,' Carlyle told Macvey Napier. 'There is no Periodical now extant in Britain which I should so willingly write for, and publish all my Essayist Lucubrations in as the *Edinburgh Review*.' When Napier had to postpone one of his articles in 1844, G. H. Lewes responded instantly that the 'immense superiority of the *Edinburgh Review* over all other Reviews in influence, and the chance it affords a writer of being read by those readers he most desires, quite overbalances any advantages derived from immediate publication elsewhere'. The historian W. F. P. Napier expressed pleasure that his *History of the Peninsular War* was to be reviewed in the *Edinburgh* 'for to every part of the world your influence in literature extends'. When what he considered a serious misrepresentation of his father, in Bowring's *Memoirs of Jeremy Bentham*, had been given prominence in the *Edinburgh*'s review of the work, J. S. Mill demanded and received the right of reply in the following number, arguing that it was one thing to have the error occur in a book which he had not in fact read, but that 'the case is very much altered when that loose talk has received the imprimatur of the *Edinburgh Review*'.[16]

'Review writing is one of the features of modern literature,' Bagehot commented in 1855, in his article on 'The First Edinburgh Reviewers'. 'Many able people give themselves up to it.'[17] The comment would have been as applicable to the 1820s and 1830s as it was to the thriving reviewing scene of the mid-century. The comfortable links between the world of literature and the world of public life that characterized the higher journalism of the 1860s and 1870s were the legacy of the quarterlies, a situation which had been carefully nurtured by editors, contributors and proprietors from the beginning. Reviewing became an intermittent activity of men in public and professional life as well as a nearly full-time commitment for literary men, particularly those at the beginning of their careers, for whom an income from reviewing was a welcome buffer against the less certain returns of other forms of literary activity.

Quarterly reviewing in its early stages, Leslie Stephen suggested, had therefore been essentially amateur, and as such could not withstand the rigorous scrutiny of a later generation, used to higher standards of journalism. Amateurism, he reflected, had both its strengths and weaknesses:

> An article upon politics or philosophy is, of course, better done by a professed statesman and thinker than by a literary hack; but on the other hand, a man who turns aside from politics or philosophy to do mere hackwork, does it worse than the professed man of letters. Work, taken up at odd hours to satisfy editorial importunity or add a few pounds to a narrow income, is apt to show the characteristic defects of all amateur performances. A very large part of the early numbers [of the *Edinburgh*] is amateurish in this objectionable sense. It is mere hand-to-mouth information, and is written, so to speak, with the left hand... The young gentlemen who wrote in those days have a jaunty mode of pronouncing upon all conceivable topics without even affecting to have studied the subject, which is amusing in its way and which fully explains the flimsy nature of their performance.

And how unlike the present day, Stephen added with a certain smugness at the end, when 'much of the most solid and original work of the time first appears in periodicals'.[18]

His comments were directed primarily to the early days of the *Edinburgh* and not so much to the 1830s and beyond, when Carlyle, Macaulay, MacCulloch, Hazlitt, Bulwer Lytton, William Empson, John Allen, Herman Merivale, Dionysius Lardner, James Stephen, Edwin Chadwick, Thomas Arnold, Francis Palgrave, James Spedding, Bonamy Price, Abraham Hayward, and a host of other able reviewers established their own reputations as well as reinforcing that of the Review by their contributions. The amateurism which

Stephen deplored was equivalent to the slapdash, the whimsical, the irresponsible, and the superficial, charges which could indeed be levelled at both the *Edinburgh* and the *Quarterly* at certain periods of their existence.

Looked at in another way, the so-called amateurism of the quarterlies was a strength. For Bagehot they represented a healthy, non-specialist view of literature on the part of reviewers and readers alike. There was a new desire among the reading public, he maintained, to be able to consider and to be informed on a broad range of subjects, rather than just on their professional interests. The quarterly review format had come into existence to supply just such a need:

> It is indeed a peculiarity of our times, that we must instruct so many persons. On politics, on religion, on all less important topics still more, everyone thinks himself competent to think, — in some casual manner does think, — to the best of our means must be taught to think rightly... We must speak to the many so that they will listen, — that they will understand.

The solid, expansive scholarship of the past could not accommodate this modern need nor could the small-scale essays of the *Spectator* and the *Tatler* model:

> The modern man must be told what to think — shortly, no doubt — but he *must* be told it. The essay-like criticism of modern times is about the length which he likes. The *Edinburgh Review*, which began the system, may be said to be, in this country, the commencement on large topics of suitable views for sensible persons.[19]

For Bagehot, the Scottish education system, with its broad range of subjects and healthy injection of philosophy, produced the ideal reviewer — critical, analytical, disputatious when necessary, and avowedly non-specialist. Numerous examples, both Scottish and non-Scottish, could be produced to illustrate the quintessential reviewer, whatever his background and education. But one fact stands out. The quarterly reviewer, and the quarterly reader, were part of a far more homogeneous culture than the twentieth century can believe possible. The crucial assumption of each number of a quarterly was that all areas of knowledge were not only accessible, but potentially of interest and part of one's general cultivation. The comparative accessibility of scientific writing and of political economy, at least in terms of style and language, to take two examples of areas now regarded as highly specialized, may have made reviewing for a lay audience less daunting than would be the case today. But the sheer intellectual stamina required to read two hundred and fifty to three hundred pages of a quarterly across a range of subjects, and to read intelligently and thoughtfully, seems incredible, even to the most assiduous of modern periodical readers.

Equally impressive was the stamina of the practised reviewer, who might well review across a range of subjects. John Wilson Croker, one of the *Quarterly*'s mainstays, was known to produce as many as four reviews in a single number, while also an active Member of Parliament and Secretary of the Admiralty. He was the Review's main political writer but he also reviewed history, biography and literature. Henry Brougham, who was associated with the *Edinburgh* from the beginning, contributed steadily from the first number until the mid-1840s. He too had a broad range of interests, which manifested themselves in his remarkably prolific and varied career as well as in his reviewing. He contributed as many as six articles to a single number at his peak of activity, his subjects including politics, economics, legal and social questions, history and biography. Jeffrey himself was perhaps the best example of the non-specialist reviewer. He wrote at an enormous pace — contributing at one point an average of three articles per number to the first twenty-six numbers of the Review, while keeping his legal career going at the same time. Besides the famous literary criticism, his subjects included biology, metaphysics, politics and morals, all of which he considered himself competent to tackle. Amateurism may well have produced thinness, as Stephen alleged, and the work of Croker, Brougham and Jeffrey would have answered to this charge from time to time. But the homogeneity of the society in which the quarterlies flourished, the close links between literature and public and professional life and the cohesiveness of the intelligentsia were enviable aspects of their success which were lost to a later generation of journalists and a later era of periodicals.

That the quarterlies were read, and avidly, is undeniable. Circulation figures, which admittedly convey only a partial picture of the total reading pattern, show a run of between 12,000 and 14,000 for the

Quarterly and slightly less for the *Edinburgh*. John Murray's ledgers for the 1830s reveal a print run for the *Quarterly* of between 9,000 and 10,000 for a period up to the mid-1840s. Press historians remind us that sales figures and print runs can never provide a total picture of readership, particularly for publications which cost as much as six shillings, and which were as likely to be read in clubs, libraries, reading rooms and common rooms as in private homes. The actual readership is likely to have been vastly in excess of the *Quarterly*'s 14,000, at least until the 1840s when, in general, the quarterlies' readership and their influence began a slow but inexorable decline.[20]

Carlyle's implicit grumble, in his letter to Mill, that Reviews were dominated by vested interests and that the unattached reviewer found it difficult to find a congenial home, represented a popular view of the quarterlies, and of the higher reaches of the periodical press generally. Introducing the Saint Simonian Gustave d'Eichthal to the reviewing scene of the 1830s, Mill pressed the advantages of being attacked from a variety of entrenched positions with nice irony:

> Now since you have been violently attacked already by Southey, in so widely circulated a work as the *Quarterly Review* & mentioned in several newspapers of large circulation as a set of dreamers and visionaries, it is desirable that you should be attacked a great deal more, & by a great variety of persons, in order that being attacked on all sides, your doctrine may have all its sides laid bare and divulged. Each person in pointing out the things which *he* dislikes, will shew to some other person that there are things which *he* would like. While you are only attacked as anarchists & levellers, you will excite no attention here, but when you come to be represented by A as anarchists; by B as absolutists; by C as levellers; by D as hierarchs; by E as infidels; by F as mystical religionists; by G as sentimentalists; by H as metaphysicians & political economists; & so forth; the public will see that an absurdity which has so many different faces, cannot be quite an absurdity; or at least, that it is an absurdity unlike others, & worth noting.

Arnold was to put the case more forcibly as late as 1863 in his essay 'The Function of Criticism at the Present Time':

> We have the *Edinburgh Review*, existing as an organ of the old Whigs, and for as much play of the mind as may suit its being that; we have the *Quarterly Review*, existing as an organ of the Tories, and for as much play of mind as may suit its being that; we have the *British Quarterly Review*, existing as an organ of the political Dissenters, and for as much play of mind as may suit its being that; we have *The Times*, existing as an

organ of the common, satisfied, well-to-do Englishman, and for as much play of mind as may suit its being that.[21]

Party affiliation and allegiances of other sorts undoubtedly played some part in determining the readership of the quarterlies, but the general sense, derived from letters, diaries, memoirs and the perspective of editors and contributors, is that rather than being highly compartmentalized and segmented, as Arnold had alleged, into Whigs, Tories, Nonconformists, and High Churchmen, the readership of the quarterlies was a relatively unified group, intelligent, educated, middle-class and serious-minded, which read widely and discriminatingly, sampling more than one Review. A comparison with the modern reader of a daily newspaper, devoted to one paper and taking on the acknowledged attitudes of a *Times* reader, a *Telegraph* or a *Guardian* reader, is not borne out by the available evidence.

Henry Crabb Robinson, whose diary, in the words of its twentieth-century editor, 'represents the intelligent reader of his long day' (1775–1867), presents an interesting profile of a quarterly reader virtually from their beginning and carrying on intermittently through to his death in 1867. Crabb Robinson read both the *Edinburgh* and the *Quarterly* on a regular basis, sometimes at the Athenaeum, sometimes spending a day in bed reading a recent number, sometimes buying it abroad to read while travelling. His reading was entirely apolitical. The *Edinburgh* and the *Quarterly* were adjuncts of his literary, not his political, life. He compared their responses to current books as they came out. He swapped his own reactions to particular reviews with his friends. He held a grudge against the *Edinburgh* for its treatment of Wordsworth well into the 1830s and confronted Jeffrey with it when they met for the first time in 1835. He deplored the *Quarterly*'s review of Madame d'Arblay's *Memoirs* (see p. 67), and its malignity towards Thomas Moore. He relished Hazlitt's review of Horace Walpole's letters, the style of which he thought had furnished the model for the *Edinburgh*.

He met Macaulay as early as 1826, at a dinner at the elder James Stephen's, pronouncing him 'one of the most promising of the rising generation I have seen for a long time'. Sydney Smith, whom he finally met in 1836, was a disappointment: 'His manner is that of a person who knows that a joke is expected'. He read Southey's *Essays* when they were reprinted from the *Quarterly* in 1832 and found nothing in them to disapprove of. He spent a congenial evening with

Southey chatting on all kinds of subjects and concluded at the end that he could not greatly differ from him about anything, 'his greatest fault being that, like almost all, he is one-sided'.[22]

Crabb Robinson's partisanship, when it was occasionally manifested, was based on personality and literary preference, never on ideology. As well as the *Edinburgh* and the *Quarterly*, he read *Blackwood's*, the *Athenaeum*, the *Westminster*, the *Examiner*, and he noted the establishment of new periodicals like the *Foreign Quarterly*. The periodical press, and the quarterlies in particular, were inseparable from the literary life of which he was a discerning observer as well as a peripheral participant.

By contrast, Charles Greville's *Memoirs*, which cover much the same period, are those of a shrewd observer of the political scene. He too read the *Edinburgh*, the *Quarterly* and the *Foreign Quarterly* but his constant point of reference was *The Times*. The quarterlies were on the periphery of his world, rather than central to it, as they were with Crabb Robinson. But, as with Robinson, Greville appears to espouse no particular Review over another. An article by Lockhart in the *Quarterly* for March 1832 attacked some of his friends and at their behest Greville published a pamphlet in response — entitled, interestingly, 'Letter to Lockhart...'. The *Memoirs* are full of gossip and speculation about Brougham, whose immense talents coupled with irreparable flaws Greville clearly found fascinating. He reported a story of Brougham's apparently 'losing' two articles forwarded to him to be handed to Jeffrey for insertion in the *Edinburgh*. Like Robinson he dined with various quarterly figures — Moore, Sydney Smith, and Macaulay. Unlike Robinson, he found Macaulay both disappointing and disagreeable when he met him in 1833:

> All [he] says, all that he writes, exhibits his great powers and astonishing information, but I don't think he is agreeable. It is more than society requires, and not exactly of the kind; his figure, face, voice and manner are all bad; he astonishes and instructs; he sometimes entertains; seldom amuses, and still seldom pleases. He wants variety, elasticity, gracefulness; his is a roaring torrent and not a meandering stream of talk. I believe we should all of us have been glad to exchange some of his sense for some of Sydney Smith's nonsense.[23]

What emerges from both diaries is the sense in which the milieu of the Reviews produced its stars, and also how long-lived their reputations were. Jeffrey and Sydney Smith figure equally in Greville and Crabb Robinson's worlds — the older generation whose reputations went before them, and for whom, in some cases, the reality could not quite match up to the legend. Macaulay's reputation was in the making as early as 1826, according to Crabb Robinson. Significantly, Greville regarded him and also Croker as political rather than literary luminaries. The *Memoirs* give graphic accounts of their collisions in the House of Commons during the Reform Bill debates of 1831.

For his own generation Macaulay epitomized the heights of reviewing fame and set a standard almost impossible of emulation. James Stephen, the son of Crabb Robinson's host in 1826, responded somewhat nervously to Macvey Napier's invitation to contribute to the *Edinburgh* in 1838 with the comment that he had been accustomed to think of the *Edinburgh* as 'an enterprise reserved for that small class of persons to which my friend McAulay [sic] belongs — if indeed he is not to be considered as forming a class by himself & apart from all other men'.[24]

Comments similar to this abound in Napier's correspondence with almost as much predictability as the less flattering comments on Croker's contributions to the *Quarterly*. The flow of adulation and the buzz of gossip tend to obscure one important feature of the quarterlies. The articles were unsigned and no name apart from the publisher's and sometimes the printer's appeared on any issue.

The underlying assumption of anonymity was the production of a corporate voice and corporate responsibility, with the editor ultimately assuming responsibility for unanimity or the illusion of it. According to Samuel Smiles, in his *Memoir of John Murray*, William Gifford, the *Quarterly*'s first editor, held that 'inviolable secrecy' was one of the prime functions of an editor. Croker in 1823 reminded Murray of the necessity of 'absolute secrecy' on the point of authorship: 'If you were to publish such names as Cohen and Croker and Collinson and Coleridge the magical We would have little effect and your Review would be absolutely despised.'[25]

To what extent the editorial 'we' was ever more than a widely acknowledged fiction is difficult to gauge. The code of anonymity appears to have been as much honoured in the breach as in the observance. The authorship of major articles or articles by well-known contributors was an open secret in literary and political circles and the trading of such information a regular ingredient of literary gossip, as contemporary correspondence regularly testified.

In principle the editorial 'we' was an acknowledgement of firm editorial control and the subordination of individual personalities and personal display to that control. But Jeffrey's favourite analogy of himself as 'a Feudal monarch who really had but slender control over his barons' was more than a pleasing joke. The welding together of egocentric, opinionated and at times rebellious contributors made an editor's task a headache from time to time. But it was also part of the challenge.

With the advent of signed articles from the late 1850s — *Macmillan's Magazine* admitted signatures in 1859 — the monthly segment of the periodical press transformed itself into what John Morley termed the 'open pulpit'. The abandonment of anonymity led, he claimed, to a greater freedom of discussion, particularly in complex areas like religious belief, and it contributed too, he believed, to a higher standard of writing. But the role of the editor had unquestionably diminished and there was as much opportunity for insincerity under the new system as under the old.

Most observers would have agreed with Morley that there was a 'monstrous charlatanry' about the old editorial 'we'.[26] There would have been agreement, too, that there was as much temptation to insincerity with signed articles as with unsigned ones, in other words an impulse to say what was expected of one rather than what one might have wanted to say under cover of anonymity. For this very reason, weeklies like the *Spectator*, the *Athenaeum* and the *Saturday Review* chose to retain anonymity until the end of the century, in order to permit men in public and professional life to air possibly controversial or unexpected opinions in their pages. It also gave the editors of the weeklies, as they well knew, greater control over their publications.

Few editors were able to achieve the absolute secrecy sought by Gifford and advised by Croker. Their own appointments were the subject of endless gossip and speculation and the identity of their major contributors, particularly those with easily recognizable styles or known subject areas, appears to have been common knowledge in reviewing circles and beyond. Crabb Robinson's diaries are full of references to articles by Carlyle, Hazlitt, Croker and Southey as well as ecstatic references to virtually all of Macaulay's essays within days of publication. And Crabb Robinson was by no means unique. J. A. Stuart, editor of the *Courier*, and a friend of Macvey Napier, soon put him wise as to the impossibility of maintaining even temporary secrecy over authorship:

> Every man knew the writer of the Bank article [J. R. MacCulloch, May 1833] because only one man could write it. It was easy to guess the others, just as Mr. Black of the *Chronicle* guessed the Chancellor [Brougham] to be the author of the No Ballot article. Don't be so sensitive. Even I knew Macaulay in the notice of Ld. Mahon.[27]

Brougham complained to Napier in 1836 that 'an unfortunate practice has arisen in the Liberal press of treating all papers in the ER as if the names of the authors were appended to them', and not altogether seriously proposed the retaliation of naming the writers of newspapers. 'I never have any reliance on authorship being concealed,' Henry Cockburn wrote nervously to Napier after writing a sensitive political article while poised to accept a minor office in the Whig government of 1830. Later he was to refuse to write on political subjects altogether because of his inside knowledge and the likelihood of discovery.[28] It was a constant source of annoyance to J. W. Croker that his name was automatically ascribed to every political article in the *Quarterly*, including those he had not written, a kind of perverse disadvantage of anonymity. There were obvious risks in writing politically sensitive articles but for the astute there were also advantages, and for as many authors who wrote in the hope of concealment there were others who wrote in the expectation of publicity.

The open secrets and surmises about authorship were sometimes wrong, which suggests that the circles who were in on the secrets were smaller than is sometimes thought. The young Disraeli derived great delight in repeating Lockhart's comment on reading the *Edinburgh* for August 1825: 'Well, they may say what they like, but no man can write like Jeffrey on poetry. The article on Milton in the new number is the finest thing we have had for years.' Having boasted of this knowledge to Archibald Constable and been put straight, Disraeli returned to London with 'a sort of literary secret', as he termed it, and professed a lasting low opinion of Lockhart's literary discrimination as a result. Even more surprisingly, Jeffrey failed to recognize Hazlitt's hand in the first number brought out by Napier (October 1829), pronouncing the author of an article on William Ellery Channing as 'not a first rate man — a clever writer enough, but not deep or judicious or even very fair', which must have proved a momentary embarrassment at least.[29]

Once a kind of quasi-anonymity became the norm, the ideal of a corporate voice, the 'magical we' as Croker described it, became harder to achieve. Sir George Murray, an associate of the Duke of Wellington, who was engaged to review the Duke's *Despatches* for the *Edinburgh* in 1838, shrewdly summarized the new consensus when he observed that 'a real secrecy' was now seldom obtainable but that 'a sort of nominal incognito by the absence of any direct acknowledgement of authorship' might sometimes be a matter of convenience to all parties.[30]

Most editors felt able to negotiate this 'nominal incognito' whereas absolute secrecy proved an impossibility. Everyone knew Macaulay's reviews, most guessed Brougham's and Southey's and thought they knew Croker's. For reviewers like Croker and Brougham who sometimes wrote as many as four articles in one number the detection rate was never perfect and attributions were often incorrectly made. Carlyle's early essays on German literature received favourable nods in the *Edinburgh* whereas 'Characteristics' in December 1831 created such an uproar that it signalled the parting of the ways between Carlyle and the Review. The discrepancy in their reception might not have been due entirely to anonymity, but it was probably one reason for it. But as Morley commented, it was impossible for any writer of real distinction to remain anonymous. If a writer in a periodical interested the public they were sure to find out who he was. Anonymity then, and its accompanying ideal of a corporate voice, had by the mid-1820s undergone a gradual erosion.

The quarterlies' dominance of the serious periodical press remained unchallenged until the 1840s. The bustle and notoriety of *Blackwood's* and the stir caused by *Fraser's* were, it was generally agreed, of a different order. So too was the impact made by weeklies like the *Athenaeum*, the *Spectator* and the *Examiner*. The quarterlies continued to make reputations and to serve as an entree to the world of serious literature for young writers as well as providing a forum for established writers, scholars, theologians, politicians, scientists, diplomats and even civil servants who made convenient use of anonymity.

John Clive, in his book *Scotch Reviewers*, a study of the first thirteen years of the *Edinburgh Review*, nicely summarized the snares of writing about periodical literature — the danger of according excessive significance to an article dashed off on the spur of the moment; the folly of seeing a grand plan or a carefully moderated policy where none existed; and, more significantly, the need to see the periodical in context in the fullest sense of the term in order to understand its influence and to appreciate the external forces, social, political and even psychological which helped to shape an article or an entire number. Perhaps, Clive suggested, only half in jest, it is impossible to write about a periodical publication at all without writing a complete history, not only of the life and times of its contributors, but of its readers as well.

This study is an attempt to confront this particular problem — again to use Clive's words — to surround the 'dry bones' of the periodicals themselves 'with the flesh of personal context and contemporary setting'.[31] I have endeavoured, to take another analogy, to analyze the 'chemistry' of a periodical publication, or more specifically, the chemistry of the *Edinburgh* and *Quarterly* Reviews in the period immediately following the celebrated early decades. I have taken up the story, in each case, at the point when the founding editor retired. Francis Jeffrey relinquished his control of the *Edinburgh* in the summer of 1829 to become Dean of the Faculty of Advocates and, soon after, Lord Advocate. William Gifford retired from the *Quarterly* because of ill health at the end of 1823, to be succeeded in the first instance by John Taylor Coleridge, and then, more significantly, by John Gibson Lockhart in the autumn of 1825. In both cases the second editorial generation ushered in a new era of reviewing, a period which was in some ways less spectacular, less overtly partisan in the political sense, and ultimately sounder in terms of the quality of reviewing.

My concern has been the construction of context, the myriad elements, personal, social, political and technical, which were woven into a single review, an individual number, and ultimately the run of a decade or more. My focus has been primarily on the 1830s, the last decade in which the quarterlies maintained their political authority and their overall critical influence. As the power of the newspaper press grew, that of the quarterlies, politically, at least, declined. Paradoxically the quality of their general criticism remained high and even improved in the 1840s and 1850s, but by the early 1840s their great days were over. The power to influence events and to make reputations had gone. The quarterlies were a spent force, elbowed out in the political sphere by the newspapers as they were to be elbowed out finally as organs of critical opinion by the weeklies and monthlies of the 1850s and 1860s.

Notes

1. William Hazlitt, 'On Respectable People', The Plain Speaker, *Works*, Centenary Edition, 21 vols. ed P.P. Howe, (London: Dent, 1930-4), XII, 365. Walter Bagehot, 'The First Edinburgh Reviewers', *Literary Studies* I (London: Longman's, Green and Co., 1884), 1.
2. Hazlitt, 'The Periodical Press', *Works*, XVI, 220.
3. *The Letters of Thomas Babington Macaulay*, edited by Thomas Pinney, 6 vols. (Cambridge: Cambridge University Press, 1974), III, 245; cited hereafter as Macaulay, *Letters*.
4. Thomas Carlyle, 'Characteristics', *Essays*, 4 Vols (London: Chapman and Hall, 1857), III, 19. The comment about Byron's regarding the reviewer and the poet as equals was presumably a reference to 'English Bards and Scotch Reviewers', which had been regularly reissued since 1809. See the British Library Catalogue for details.
5. *The Collected Letters of Thomas and Jane Welsh Carlyle*, edited by Charles Richard Sanders and Kenneth J. Fielding, Duke-Edinburgh edition, 12 vols (Durham, NC: Duke University Press, 1977-85), VII, 70-1, cited hereafter as Carlyle, *Letters*.
6. Derek Roper, *Reviewing before the Edinburgh 1788–1802* (Newark, NJ: University of Delaware Press, 1978), p.36.
7. Henry Cockburn, *The Life of Lord Jeffrey with a Selection from his Correspondence*, 2 vols (Edinburgh: Adam and Charles Black, 1852), I, 131. Cockburn (1779–1854) was a prominent Scottish Whig, a life long friend of Jeffrey's, and of the *Edinburgh Review* generally. He was also a leading advocate, and was made Solicitor-General for Scotland in the Whig government of 1830. In 1834 he became Judge of the Court of Session.
8. Roper claims that the connections between the original Reviews and booksellers were exaggerated. The *Monthly Review* had been old Whig in its affiliations; the *Critical* had been Tory and later Foxite but political affiliation had not been a prominent feature of the original Reviews. See Roper, Ch. I, pp.19–48.
9. Cockburn, *Life*, I, 133.
10. Cockburn, *Life*, I, 280.
11. Quoted by Andrew Lang, *The Life and Letters of John Gibson Lockhart*, 2 vols (London: John C. Nimmo, 1897), I, 365, 367.
12. Lang, II, 51–2.
13. John Gross, *The Rise and Fall of the Man of Letters* (London:

Weidenfeld and Nicolson, 1969), p.10. Napier Correspondence, British Library, Add. MSS. 34615, f.253.

14. BL Add. MSS. 34615, f.95; *Selection from the Correspondence of the late Macvey Napier*, edited by his son (London: Macmillan and Co., 1879), p.21. Hereafter cited as *Napier*.

15. *The Later Letters of John Stuart Mill 1849–1873*, edited by Francis E.Mineka and D.N. Lindley, 4 vols, *The Collected Works of John Stuart Mill*, vols XIV–XVII (London: Routledge, 1972), XIV, 63.

16. Carlyle, *Letters*, V, 310-11; Napier, pp.463, 340-1; *The Earlier Letters of John Stuart Mill 1812–1848*, 2 vols, edited by Francis E. Mineka, *The Collected Works of John Stuart Mill* vols XII–XIII (London: Routledge, 1963), XIII, 601.

17. Bagehot, *Literary Studies*, I, 2.

18. Leslie Stephen, 'The First Edinburgh Reviewers', *Hours in a Library*, 3 vols (London: Smith Elder, 1899), II, 248-9, 269.

19. Bagehot, *Literary Studies* I, 3–4, 6.

20. Samuel Smiles, *A Publisher and his Friends: Memoir and Correspondence of John Murray*, 2 vols (London: John Murray, 1897), II, 39. Apart from the Murray ledgers, which cover the period January 1829 to July 1846, hard evidence of circulation figures for either quarterly is difficult to find. Scott, *Letters*, X, 414, 420–1, claimed 12,000 as the circulation of the *Quarterly* in 1828, and that the *Edinburgh* did not sell 6,000. His *Letters*, II, 103, claimed 9,000 as the circulation of the *Edinburgh* in 1808–9. Mrs Gordon, *Christopher North: A Memoir of John Wilson* 2 vols (Edinburgh: Edmonston and Douglas, 1862), II, 71 quoted Lockhart's claim that the *Quarterly* sold 14,000 in the early years of his editorship. On sales figures and influence, see Stephen Koss, *The Rise and Fall of the Political Press in Britain* (London: Hamish Hamilton, 1981), I, 24–5.

21. *The Earlier Letters of John Stuart Mill 1812–1848*, *Collected Works*, XII, 90; Matthew Arnold, 'The Function of Criticism at the Present Time', *Essays in Criticism*, First Series (London: Macmillan, 1865), pp.19–20.

22. *Henry Crabb Robinson on Books and their Writers* ed. Edith J. Morley, 3 vols (London: Dent, 1938), I, v, 229, 341; II, 493; I, 431.

23. *The Greville Memoirs: A Journal of the Reigns of King George IV, King William IV and Queen Victoria*, by Charles C. F. Greville, ed. Henry Reeve, 8 vols (London: Longmans, Green, 1888), III, 36.

24. BL Add. MSS. 34619, f.8.

25. Samuel Smiles, *Memoir of John Murray*, II, 57–8.

26. John Morley, 'Memorials of a Man of Letters', in *Nineteenth Century Essays*, ed. Peter Stansky (London: University of Chicago Press, 1970), p.272.

27. BL Add. MSS. 34614, f.29.

28. BL Add. MSS. 34617, f.355; 34614, f.410.

29. W. F. Monypenny and G. E. Buckle, *The Life of Disraeli*, 2 vols rev. ed. (London: John Murray, 1929), I, 81–2; Napier, p.70.

30. BL Add. MSS. 34619, f.137.
31. John Clive, *Scotch Reviewers: The Edinburgh Review 1802–1815* (London: Faber, 1957), p.12.

Chapter 2

THE *EDINBURGH REVIEW* AFTER JEFFREY

Jeffrey's departure in June 1829 marked a new era in the *Edinburgh*'s history. The Review was at a difficult stage in its fortunes. It had weathered twenty-seven years of critical battles, including the founding of the *Quarterly Review* in 1809 and more recently, in 1824, the establishment of the *Westminster*. Politically it had been in opposition for Jeffrey's entire editorship, apart from the brief Ministry of all the Talents in 1806–7. It would not have been surprising if it had begun to run out of steam.

'Can you not lay your hands on some clever young man who would write for us,' Jeffrey had written to John Allen at Holland House in 1825. 'The original supporters of the work are getting old and either too busy, or too stupid, to go on comfortably; and here the young men are mostly Tories.'[1] Two new recruits had emerged, although not as a result of Allen's intervention: the young Macaulay, just down from Cambridge, whose essay on Milton in the August 1825 number had dazzled literary circles, and Carlyle, whose essay on Burns appeared in December 1828, followed by his 'Signs of the Times' in Jeffrey's last number (June 1829). They joined another young London-based reviewer in whom Jeffrey placed great trust, William Empson, a shy, vague, somewhat eccentric professor of English law at the East India College at Haileybury.[2] These three represented the *Edinburgh*'s second generation, and effectively its future.

Jeffrey's departure at a point when it had begun to seem possible that the established opposition journal might be translated into a government Review left its supporters understandably jittery. Rumours as to the succession abounded and also a contrary suggestion that the Review was to be given up. According to his sister, the job was offered to Macaulay, who accepted on condition that the centre of operations was moved to London, but Brougham then intervened and the matter foundered on the question of location. More improbably, it was rumoured that Croker was a possible successor, no doubt based on the erroneous assumption that, like other followers of Canning, he was to join the Whigs.[3] Neither rumour appears to have had much substance. The issue of Edinburgh as the place of publication was likely to have remained a sticking point at this juncture, making an Edinburgh candidate the only real possibility. The job was eventually offered to Macvey Napier, an academic with known Whiggish views, who at one time had been a regular though scarcely prolific contributor. Napier was 53, three years younger than Jeffrey. Through his friendship with Archibald Constable he had become the editor of the supplement to the sixth edition of the *Encyclopædia Britannica*, and then editor of the seventh edition. He was also Librarian to the Writers to the Signet, and the holder of the newly established Chair of Conveyancing in the University. It was a safe, but uninspired choice.

The news, when it broke, was a predictable anti-climax. Carlyle's friend Henry Inglis, an Edinburgh lawyer, claimed that Jeffrey had sold his birthright for a mess of pottage, and groaned: 'What a poor, worm-eaten, touchwood structure will it now dwindle into under the contracting influence of its mongrel Editor; — the mere paltry engine of a local party, instead of the voice of a true man to a free land'.[4]

Others no doubt shared his disquiet, but the Review's faithful were being rallied behind the scenes, mainly by Jeffrey. He cajoled Empson into declaring his allegiance to Napier early in August, and Empson in turn promised to deliver Macaulay. Empson 'has my orders as well as yours, and does not fail men in the very heat of the battle,' Jeffrey told Napier. 'At all hazards you must keep Macaulay and Empson, whatever may become of Brougham,' J. R. Mac-Culloch, the political economist and a regular reviewer, warned him at an early stage. 'The assistance of the former is of the highest importance, that of the latter you will find to be of very little or rather of no value.' It was to be some years before the truth of this advice was fully borne in upon Napier.

Jeffrey continued to direct the October 1829 number, officially Napier's first, from his holiday residence in Ayrshire, suggesting the order of the articles, making arrangements with the printers, and apologizing for 'the last agonies of an expiring Editor'. He had been 'bent upon dying upon my feet', he told Napier.[5] Brougham remained strangely coy, but Jeffrey counselled patience, and at the eleventh hour no less than four articles were hastily dispatched for Napier's first number, far more than were needed, but Jeffrey cautioned against refusal. Brougham coquettishly insisted that his authorship remain a secret, an absurd demand given the regularity of his contributions hitherto and their unmistakable style. Napier acquiesced in the charade in the hope of securing Brougham's support. Hindsight must have made him question the wisdom of this.

Both diffident and innately conservative by nature, Napier was nevertheless 'not altogether a novice', as he put it, in editorial matters.[6] One of his first measures was to let it be known that he favoured shorter articles of a sheet (sixteen pages of print) or a sheet and a half, to restore the variety of subjects that the *Edinburgh* had contained in its early days. This immediately brought protests from MacCulloch and Macaulay among others, the former maintaining that any attempt to act upon such a system would ruin the Review. If the *Edinburgh Review* was to succeed it must be thought to be not only clever but profound, and it was difficult to be profound, he thought, when chafing against restrictions in length. Macaulay suggested a combination of long and short articles by way of compromise, and the introduction of a 'lively appercu' (sic) of the works which had appeared during the quarter at the end of each number, in the manner of the *Monthly Review*.[7] True to his word, Napier's first number contained fifteen articles, in contrast to the standard nine of the preceding issues, and future issues settled down to an average of between eleven and thirteen articles.

Napier was determined to be an activist editor. More experience might have taught him to choose someone other than Macaulay on whom to begin his well-intentioned excisions. Macaulay's article, 'The Utilitarian Theory of Government and the "greatest happiness principle" ' (October 1829), the last instalment in a well-publicized debate between the *Edinburgh* and the *Westminster*, appeared with substantial portions missing, due to a printer's error, and others altered.

Macaulay's protests to Napier were polite, but to Jeffrey and Empson he was furious, claiming that the alterations were more numerous in this one article than in all thirteen articles he had written for Jeffrey put together. 'It is my decided conviction that you cannot go on without these men,' Jeffrey warned Napier. 'Mac is a man of excellent feeling & good nature,' Empson wrote, reassuringly; 'He has all the confidence wh belongs inseparably to such great Talents... I am sure he will draw vigorously & honestly with us — but a little Management is required in such a case as with a favourite Actor on the Stage.'[8]

The matter soon blew over, and Macaulay wrote affably to Napier hoping that he would not conclude from what had passed between them that he was irritable or unreasonable. But the incident was salutary, and a clear indication of the changing climate of the quarterlies. Anonymity notwithstanding, it was an age of 'names', and without them an editor, especially a new editor, was at risk. Napier's misfortune, in a way, was that he had not one star, but two, and that they were antipathetic.

Brougham's position within the *Edinburgh*'s hierarchy had never been an easy one. Very much the fourth member of the original quartet who founded the Review, he had never entirely been assimilated by Smith, Horner and Jeffrey.[9] His relations with the latter had always been cordial, but the excesses and unpredictability which characterized other aspects of his professional life marked and marred his connections with the Review. Jeffrey had always handled Brougham carefully, and presented him to Napier as one who had to be deftly managed. His initial coyness was, Jeffrey thought, simply a way of waiting to size up the number, after which he would either 'fly off' or 'cordially come round'. If a rupture arose, it would be easier and better to throw him off, rather than the Review.[10]

At the time of Napier's accession Brougham had more or less reached the height of his political power. He was the acknowledged unofficial leader of the Whig opposition in Parliament at a point when the party was poised for government. His 'elevation' to the Lord Chancellorship in November 1830 was seen by some as a defeat and a way of removing him effectively from influence in the Commons.[11] Nevertheless it was the first high office he had held and it strengthened his position with the Review.

His early relations with Macaulay did not run smoothly. The gap of a generation between himself and the brilliant and meteorically successful son of one of his oldest friends fuelled considerable envy, particularly as Macaulay's influence within the Review was visibly growing. The fact that Brougham was of Zachary Macaulay's generation and a friend of his weighed considerably with the younger man and led him to tolerate behaviour which he otherwise would not have done.

At the outset their relations were those of the great man graciously patronizing a young recruit. The first real clash came in the summer of 1830. In July Brougham made a speech on slavery which he claimed that Macaulay had promised to review as part of an article on abolition. Macaulay bristled with indignation, claiming Brougham to be 'out of his wits', and declaring his abhorrence of puffing the Review's own contributors. At the same time he announced his imminent departure for France, where he hoped to write an extensive article on the current political situation, prompted by his fascination with the recent revolution. Brougham unfortunately had the same intention and instructed Napier early in September to 'send off your countermand to Macaulay', stating peremptorily that the French situation was crucial to the next session of Parliament and that he could trust no one with it but himself.

Macaulay was both hurt and resentful. 'I always knew that in every association, literary or political, Brougham would wish to domineer. I knew also that no Editor of the *Edinburgh Review* could, without risking the ruin of the publication, resolutely oppose the demands of a man so able and so powerful,' he wrote to Napier. It was for this reason that he had contemplated giving up writing for the Review when Jeffrey left. 'I know that Brougham dislikes me, and I have not the slightest doubt that he feels great pleasure at having taken this subject out of my hands, and at having made me understand — as I do now most clearly understand — how far my services are rated below his.' He would not continue to make an effort, or sacrifices, for a journal which lay under 'an intolerable dictation'. Empson once again stepped in as peacemaker and within a month a more accommodating letter from Macaulay indicated that he would continue to write for the Review. To Empson, however, he confided that his first concession was his last, and Empson duly warned Napier that 'we must mind our P's and Q's'.[12] This incident, in 1830, was to set the stage for the principal events of the *Edinburgh*'s history for the next ten years. It was ultimately to become a contest for ascendancy between Brougham and Macaulay, with Napier in the middle. The first game went unquestionably to Brougham. But Macaulay was to have his revenge.

With the formation of Grey's ministry in November 1830 neither had time for squabbling. Brougham's appointment to the Lord Chancellorship generated suspicions that he might be forced to withdraw from the Review. 'Our Lord Chancellor will do little more for us, I suspect,' Macaulay predicted,[13] but Brougham contributed a total of fifteen articles in the four years of his chancellorship, a steady flow interrupted only in the numbers for December 1831 and April and July 1832, which occurred at the height of Parliamentary activity over the Reform Bill. His contributions were almost entirely on current political issues: 'The Ministry and the State of the Parties' (July 1830), 'The General Election and the Ministry' (October 1830), 'Reform and the Ministry' (March 1831), 'The Dissolution and the General Election' (June 1831), 'House of Lords—Reform' (September 1831). They invariably arrived at the last minute, often preceded by instructions to Napier to hold off publication for several days until a particular question was resolved, vital information secured, or the highest sources consulted. Proofs were to be returned the following day, preferably overnight, and the entire Review was then declared ready for the press. If Napier resented such high-handedness, at this stage he gave no sign of it.

The reviews were greeted with some scepticism among the faithful. 'Brougham's articles are universally abused. They have touched you,' MacCulloch insisted. Empson was frankly nervous about Brougham's renewed vigour for political articles. 'Knowing what to do with such an article...coming from such a quarter is the most difficult part of your responsibilities,' he wrote after being pressed to secrecy regarding Brougham's July 1830 article on 'the Ministry and the State of the Parties'.[14]

With the coming to power of the Whigs there was a general sense among the Review's hierarchy of having at last come into their own as a political journal. The daily correspondence hummed with political news, both rumour and fact. Every step in the tortuous passage of the Reform Bill was reported, usually by Empson in London to Napier in Edinburgh, but also by contributors with political connections who were anxious to pass on the latest gossip.

Macaulay's almost overnight success as an orator in the House of Commons was observed with personal pride by the Review's inner circle. He had been re-elected for Calne in August 1830 after the dissolution of Parliament, having been first elected in February. He made his first speech on the Reform Bill in March 1831 and another in July, and he continued to speak throughout the winter session of

1831–2, speeches which increased his already soaring reputation. 'He outdid himself on Tuesd[ay]. I staid to hear him. He is a most extraordinary being,' Empson reported to Napier.[15]

Macaulay became a member of the Board of Control in June 1832 and its Secretary in December. At this point he announced to Napier that the only time he could reserve for the Review was before breakfast, and that he proposed to rise at five to begin work. Only occasionally, until the spring of 1833, did he fail to produce an article for each number.

To Macaulay, unlike Brougham, writing for the *Edinburgh* represented the antithesis of his political life. G. O. Trevelyan, his nephew and biographer, noted that from a very early age 'public affairs divided his thoughts with literature, and, as he grew to manhood, began more and more to divide his aspirations'.[16] He deliberately chose history and literature as subjects for review, and after 1831 elected never to write on current affairs. The rebuff of his proposed article on the French Revolution of 1830 possibly helped to resolve his mind against contemporary political articles. He agreed to an article on the 'Civil Disabilities of the Jews' (January 1831) and an article on the anti-Malthusian Michael Sadler's *Law of Population* (July 1830) with a sequel in January 1831, but after that his subjects were either literary or historical: Moore's *Life of Lord Byron* (June 1831); Croker's edition of Boswell (August 1831); Southey's edition of Bunyan (December 1831); Lord Burghley (April 1832); Mirabeau (July 1832); Lord Mahon's *History of the War of the Succession in Spain* (January 1833).

The fact that almost every article generated a buzz of controversy or adulation was part of Macaulay's aura. He dazzled his readers, as indeed he simultaneously dazzled his listeners in the House of Commons, by sheer force of words. He attracted dispute and disagreement, not only attracted it, but sometimes openly courted it.

Macaulay's work during this period was crucial to Napier. Despite his heavy Parliamentary commitments, he took a generous interest in the Review's progress. 'Macaulay and I walked home...the other day & had a long anxious talk about perfectioning the Edin [sic], in which he takes a very lively interest,' Empson reported.[17] Jeffrey's relationship with Macaulay had been that of the famous editor and elder statesman who had given an opportunity to an outstanding undergraduate and who rejoiced in his success. Napier, by contrast, was a distant provincial who was equally accommodating but who stood very much in awe of his prized contributor. Macaulay was modest and tactful in his dealings with him, suggesting new contributors like his old friend from the northern circuit, the barrister Thomas Flower Ellis, his old school friend Henry Malden, a classicist, and his brother-in-law Charles Trevelyan.

In June 1833, on one of his visits to London, Napier confided to Macaulay that a survey of some five hundred booksellers reported that the *Edinburgh* sold or did not sell according to whether or not there was an article by him. He was, in effect, carrying the Review. The strain of combining a political life with regular reviewing eventually took its toll. He complained of a stream of minor ailments: colds, a swollen face, a sore hand, an inflamed eye.

In August his fortunes took an unexpected turn. He was offered an appointment to the Supreme Council of India at a salary of £10,000 per annum. Six years in India would enable him to save half of his salary and return home with a much needed competence. It would be affectation, he told Napier, to pretend not to know that his support was vital to the Review. It was equally true that it was dangerous for a public man to withdraw wholly from the public eye. The *Edinburgh* would be an invaluable means of keeping himself in the recollection of his countrymen while abroad. There was scarcely a sentence in his recent articles, he thought, which might not as easily have been written in Calcutta as in London. And so a deal was struck by which he would send articles from India in exchange for a regular supply of recent books.

Although his autobiography gave indications to the contrary, Brougham in fact played a relatively small part in the passage of the Reform Bill. He was carefully excluded from the committee of four which drafted the Bill and he actively opposed many separate issues connected with its formulation. However, in the *Edinburgh* he gave his full support to reform and to the government. The stress of his political life at this period was intense. In the general election of 1832 the Whigs had a majority of over three hundred. Two years later the ministry was falling apart. Brougham took upon himself the task of holding the government together in those intervening years, and yet still managed time for reviewing. A series of cabinet crises, periodic threats of resignation from Lord Grey, the Irish problem and in particular the Irish Church Bill, came to a climax in the summer of

1834 with a bizarre and embarrassing speaking-tour of Scotland in support of the government, a progress described by Disraeli as 'that vagrant and grotesque apocalypse'.[18]

The articles kept coming throughout it all, usually only one in each number and with an occasional gap. But the strain was beginning to tell. The October 1834 article, 'The Last Session of Parliament', published shortly before the dismissal of Melbourne's Ministry, unwisely brought Brougham's personal vendetta against Lord Durham into the pages of the Review, and did him immense damage (see p. 94). *The Times* had begun to attack him in the summer, and his absurd blunders towards former colleagues increased the by now almost universal distrust of him. Anxiety and desperation seemed to prompt yet more feverish literary activity, and the April 1835 issue, published in the month in which he was told he was not to be a member of Melbourne's second cabinet, contained no less than six articles by him.

As political power was denied him, he clung to the Review once again as a personal forum for his own campaigns, this time conducted against the ministry which had shut him out. It was Napier who bore the brunt of Brougham's near insane anger. 'I deny our ever having vowed that we were a party Review,' he wrote in September 1835, leading up to a proposed insertion of an anti-government point. The *Edinburgh Review* was in danger of becoming a Treasury journal, he alleged two years later, with a similar intention. Any comment which could be construed as having reference to himself provoked a tirade.

Napier loyally published Brougham's proffered articles, but exasperation soon broke through his over-stretched patience. A paragraph advocating the extension of the suffrage in the political article for October 1837 was excised because Napier thought it dangerous to implicate the government in such changes. Brougham promptly accused him of toadying to the government. Napier's reply was to suggest a moratorium for a season on articles involving the present government: 'The character of the Review must be upheld. I will never change it. If it has any distinctive character as a political journal it is that of being the Whig journal.' Jeffrey supported the decision to omit the paragraph on the extension of the suffrage. Brougham protested that he was being shut out of the Review, a suggestion firmly denied by Napier:

The *Edinburgh Review* is the only journal in Britain in which, and that through me, justice has been done to you as a writer and thinker; and be

your conduct to others or to myself what it may, my own notions of
propriety make it certain that nothing disparaging to you will find
admission there, so long as my hand holds the helm.[19]

As a form of deflection Napier suggested that Brougham prepare
an edition of his speeches, which was readily accepted, and he went so
far as to negotiate terms with the Edinburgh publisher Adam Black.
The suggestion to turn his attention to non-political subjects bore
fruit in a series of historial sketches from the reigns of George III and
George IV in the issues for 1838, which were generally praised. But
even these were fraught with possible danger, as Brougham was easily
tempted to settle old scores with people connected with his early
career. A seemingly chance comment in the April 1838 article on
'George the Fourth and Queen Caroline — abuses of the Press', to
the effect that several prominent Whigs, including Lord Melbourne,
had been against reform and had then changed course upon the
formation of Lord Grey's government, sent shivers of apprehension
through Napier and Empson and resulted in a flurry of diplomatic
correspondence, culminating in a letter from Melbourne through an
intermediary to the effect that he had not taken offence, and
expressing his satisfaction that Napier would resist all future attempts
to convert the Review into an instrument of opposition to his
administration.[20]

Brougham was, however, bent on a collision course, against
Napier, against the Review and against his former colleagues. 'A mere
tongue — without a party, and without a character, in an unfriendly
audience, and with an unfriendly press — never did half so much
before,' Macaulay commented ruefully; 'As Sydney Smith says,
verily he hath a devil.'[21]

The review of the recently published *Life of Wilberforce*, also in the
April 1838 number, brought a further storm around Napier's head.
James Stephen, then Undersecretary at the Colonial Office, had
petitioned to review it the previous autumn, urged, he claimed, by the
authors, and with the added incentive of access to the sheets of the
work in advance of publication. Brougham too had his eye on the
subject but did not follow through with an offer of a review. He did,
however, protest against Stephen's doing it on the grounds of his
close family connections with Wilberforce and his circle.[22]

The review, which was written in stages as the sheets of the
five-volume work were conveyed piecemeal from the publishers, was
further delayed by Stephen's heavy commitments at the Colonial

Office, so that it did not appear until the following spring. Napier was consulted at every stage of the writing. Stephen was aware of the delicacy of his subject, flattered at having been asked to write in the *Edinburgh*, and anxious, in view of his connections, to say nothing that would give offense to the Wilberforce family. He, none the less, unwisely allowed himself to be drawn into the by now well-worn controversy between Wilberforce and his fellow anti-slavery campaigner Thomas Clarkson as to whose was the major and also the earliest contribution to the abolition of the slave trade.[23]

The second volume of the *Life* had reprinted correspondence between Wilberforce and Clarkson, over the raising of a subscription for Clarkson which presented the latter in a less than flattering light. Stephen demurely declared himself 'unable to condemn' the reprinting of the correspondence, but admitted that only a sense of duty on the part of the authors, who were Wilberforce's sons, could have justified it. He also referred to a symbolic map which Clarkson had devised to show his and Wilberforce's relative contributions to the Abolition, which was prefixed to Clarkson's *History of the Abolition of the Slave Trade* (1808). The 'map' showed four rivers, the combined force of which, it was suggested symbolically, eradicated the slave trade. One of the rivers bore Clarkson's name, with 'Wilberforce' shown as a small rivulet leading into the main channel. It was argued that Clarkson's original drawing had shown his own contribution to be an even smaller rivulet than Wilberforce's and that his name had been placed along the main stream only as the result of a printer's error.

All this would have seemed but a tempest in a teapot had not Brougham, incensed by the reference to the subscription for Clarkson and the reprinting of the correspondence, declared Stephen to be an 'enemy' of the *Edinburgh Review*, and to have reversed the Review's traditional support for Clarkson.[24] He demanded that the Review make a fulsome apology in the next issue, and he also published a pamphlet in support of Clarkson.

Stephen's review had been generally well received. Brougham, who was by now nearly crazed by his political situation and his waning hold on the Review, pressed his case. Napier, weakened by a recurrence of a bladder and kidney complaint and worn down generally, agreed to the insertion of a three page 'review' of a reprint of Clarkson's *History of the Abolition* by Brougham in the October 1838 issue, a 'review' which read as if it were by the same hand as the review of the Wilberforce biography. Stephen was justifiably annoyed and demanded the right of reply, drafting a notice for insertion in several newspapers, and at the same time refusing to write again for the *Edinburgh*, lest he bring down upon himself another attack by Brougham, scarcely the thing for a public servant to provoke. He had by this time consulted Jeffrey who urged that he be given the right of reply, and also urged upon Napier the danger of alienating so valuable a new contributor.

In the end Stephen withdrew his retort, influenced by Macaulay who hinted that he might not have been in the right either with regard to the publication of the controversial letters, or on the question of the 'map',and by the Wilberforce family, who presumably wished the row to be nipped in the bud.

Empson wrote to Napier with more kindness than conviction that his firmness and discretion would doubtless 'pilot you successfully through the shifting sands and undercurrents [with] which that great whirlpool B. does so much to perplex and damage those who come across him', but for the moment it must have seemed that Brougham was gaining the upper hand.[25]

Napier was exhausted with illness and battle fatigue. Brougham was nearly deranged by four years of public humiliation and political isolation. The correspondence between them for this period makes unpleasant reading, despite the passage of nearly a century and a half. Brougham was by turns belligerent, overbearing, insulting and conciliatory. 'I know a good deal more both of the heads and the tails of the Whig party than you possibly can do', a typical remark, would be followed by genuine surprise that Napier had been upset by a previous letter, or a series of suggestions on how to deal with a troublesome cold. At times the sheer pain of his situation broke through: 'Don't I beg of you, forget that the Government have driven me to oppose them.'[26]

Most of the Review's friends supported Napier, but most too could see the pathos of Brougham's predicament. 'He may coax or bluster, but he will not break with you,' John Allen predicted. 'Great allowance must be made for his situation.' Macaulay was quick to offer moral support on his return:

As to Brougham, I understand and feel for your embarrassments... I should say that this strange man, finding himself almost alone in the world, absolutely unconnected with either Whigs or Conservatives, and not having a single vote in either House of Parliament at his command except his own, is desirous to make the Review his organ... His wish, I imagine, is to establish in this way such an ascendancy as may enable him to drag the Review along with him to any party to which his furious passions may lead him.[27]

Napier had three choices, to break with Brougham, to admit his articles while the rest of the Review was written in quite a different tone, or to 'yield to his dictation and to let him make the Review a mere tool of his ambition and revenge'.[28] The last choice must not be permitted.

The strain was now telling on Napier. Empson reported 'all sorts of family disquiets — pecuniary embarrassments — dreadful wearing complaints which are rendered tolerable only by opium, and which in the opinion of all his friends must in a very few months end fatally.' To this was added Brougham's 'persecuting him with the malignity of a dæmon'. 'In truth, Lord Brougham is now really a Devil,' Macaulay told Ellis. 'I did not think it possible for human nature in an educated, civilized man, a man, too, of great intellect, to have become so depraved.'[29]

With Macaulay's return from India in June 1838 a new personal element entered the situation. The rising star of 1830 was now in his ascendancy while the great man was sliding rapidly into oblivion. Macaulay's smouldering resentment in 1830 had been held in check by Brougham's long standing association with his father. Struggling to fulfil his commitments to Parliament as well as to his literary work, he had remarked wittily to Napier: 'I have not the Chancellor's Encyclopædic mind. He is indeed a kind of semi-Solomon. He half knows everything from the cedar to the hyssop.' But on his return to England he wrote bitterly: 'As to Brougham's feelings towards myself, I know and have known for a long time that he hates me.' Reading Jeffrey's *Contributions to the Edinburgh* in 1843 he compared his range with his own, and with Sydney Smith's and Brougham's, reflecting, 'Brougham does one thing well, two or three things indifferently, and a hundred things detestably'.[30]

Brougham petulantly complained of Macaulay's not calling on him on his return, and pronounced him 'the second or third greatest bore in society'. Macaulay's defective style was a perpetual theme in the letters to Napier. It suffered from a 'redundancy, an over-crowding ... that almost turns one's head; for it is out of one digression into another, and each thought in each is illustrated by twenty different cases and anecdotes'. Empson too came in for criticism as 'a bad imitator of Macaulay', and a practitioner of the 'riddle and flower style, i.e. a constant saying of something fine and puzzling'.[31] Brougham became highly suspicious of Empson, particularly after his marriage to Jeffrey's daughter in June 1838, alleging at one point that there was a plan to make Empson editor of the Review, and pledging himself to do everything he could, in that case, to ruin it.

This last bit of madness arose because of the first draft of Brougham's article (October 1838) on political characters in the reigns of George III and George IV, which contained a dissertation on 'Party' and included an attack on Melbourne. Napier threatened resignation if the offensive passage was not removed. Brougham's response was that if Napier were to resign, a new *Edinburgh Review* would undoubtedly spring up, presumably under his own auspices, which would give Empson and his 'clique' strong competition. He then mercurially agreed that the article should be published without the controversial section, and pronounced himself pleased with it.[32]

By the end of 1838, almost without warning, Brougham's war with the government and his running battle with Napier suddenly subsided. He continued to write for the Review, but less frequently, and his contributions eventually ceased in April 1841. He had begun, in fact, to court the *Quarterly*. Certainly the old animosities seemed to have cooled. Lockhart, after some misgivings, admitted several articles by Brougham in 1845 and afterwards.

In the autumn of 1843 Brougham wrote confidentially to Jeffrey stating that he bore no grudge against Napier and that he wished for a reconciliation. This was by way of a prologue to a request that the *Edinburgh* review his *Political Philosophy* when it appeared, to which Napier, after some consideration, agreed. But Brougham's formal and sentimental ties with the *Edinburgh Review* had in effect been severed by the end of 1840. His painful removal from political life was mirrored by an equally painful but more gradual withdrawal from the Review.

Macaulay's Indian sojourn, despite his best intentions, produced only two articles, a review of Sir James Mackintosh's fragmentary *History of the Revolution* (July 1835), and the celebrated essay on Bacon (July 1837), but the time in India had made him even more determined to abandon politics for literature. 'All my tastes and wishes, lead me to prefer literature to politics,' he told Napier on his return.[33] The

History of England was now taking shape in his mind, and slotting into place in his future timetable. Before India the *Edinburgh* had had its valued role as a lifeline to 'literature' in contrast to the political fray. Now the Review was consciously to complement his work on the *History* and not to duplicate it. He would not choose to write an article on anything which he would have to treat again as an historian, he told Napier. Nor did he wish to write on subjects totally alien to his main interests. There were some subjects, however, that would not directly form part of his historical narrative, but with which he would have to familiarize himself in order to write that narrative, Frederick the Great being the case in point (April 1842). It was subjects like this which would be ideal material for reviews, he explained. In reply to a request from Napier to write on education shortly after he had spoken on it in the House, in 1839, he wrote: 'I have two fears, one that I may commit myself — the other, that I may repeat myself. I shall keep to history, general literature, and the merely speculative part of politics in what I write for the Review.'[34]

His determination to choose literature over politics on his return was short-lived. After a brief continental tour in the winter of 1838–9 he began work on the *History* in earnest in March 1839. In May he was invited to stand as Member of Parliament for Edinburgh. In June he was elected and in September he was offered a seat in the cabinet as Secretary for War. The old duality began again in earnest. Macaulay was in fact never to resume the intensity of reviewing which had existed prior to India. The *History of England* and the cabinet proved all too formidable rivals. But the elevation to cabinet rank brought with it a new confidence, and as Brougham's grip on the *Edinburgh* lessened so Macaulay's influence increased. By 1840 he was suggesting and securing reviewers 'from the very best sources' for sensitive political issues and arranging for their vetting by ministers and other senior figures. As his contributions gradually lessened, in the 1840s, so his importance as an adviser grew. The letters from 1840 onwards are reminiscent of those of Jeffrey, Brougham, and other senior adherents of the *Edinburgh* in 1830, commenting one by one on articles, and advising on policy. In the ten years between 1830 and 1840 the roles of Brougham and Macaulay had been reversed.

Napier had come of age as an editor through his relations with Brougham and, with some prompting from Jeffrey and Macaulay, had shown that he could be tough. His relations with Macaulay, on the other hand, after the initial skirmishes, were entirely those of the grateful and subservient editor to the Review's star contributor. His instincts, as far as the welfare of the *Edinburgh* was concerned were, in both cases, the right ones. He was much less perceptive in his dealings with Carlyle.

Jeffrey had sensed that Carlyle and Napier would find one another perplexing. In November 1829, shortly after he had given up the Review, he wrote to Carlyle:

> Napier, though his nose may have a tyrannical expression, is anxious to avail himself of your talents. But he is more alarmed at your mystical propensities than ever I am. Apply to me, whenever you are in any perplexity, as freely as if I were still in the chair of the Editor. To you, and for your sake, I will be Editor always.[35]

The office of 'Editor Emeritus' was one which Jeffrey was to discharge on many occasions throughout Napier's term, but it was particularly important with regard to Carlyle. 'There can be no more respectable vehicle for any British man's speculations than it [the *Edinburgh*] is and has always been,' Carlyle wrote to Napier the following year, expressing his willingness to write. Napier responded quickly, but Carlyle's various proposals — Moore's *Life of Byron*, Napoleon and the *Niebelungenlied* were, for a variety of reasons, refused. In March 1831 Napier published Carlyle's review of Taylor's *Historic Survey of German Poetry*, but payment was curiously slow at a point when Carlyle was desperate for money. 'Naso the Blockhead has neither paid me nor written to me,' Carlyle complained to his brother, referring to Napier's prominent nose. 'I have some thought of cutting him and his calcined caput-mortuary dead men's ashes of Whiggism.' The payment for Taylor was not made until July, Napier claiming an oversight, due to a visit to London. 'I fear you are giving reviews to works less worthy of them than my partiality makes me think the Ed. to be,' he added petulantly. 'If you really want me to preach in your Pulpit, therefore, you have only to say so,' Carlyle replied smartly.[36]

The offer of an article on Dr Johnson was refused with the explanation that Croker's Boswell had been allocated to 'a distinguished contributor', which was true. A consultation with Jeffrey about the general difficulty over assignments confirmed what

Carlyle had himself suspected, that 'he [Napier] was anxious enough to have me write, but afraid lest I committed him'. A proposed article on Luther was not refused, but strict limitations on its length made it unworkable. Napier then suggested Hope's *Thoughts on Man* and Schlegel's *Lectures* as a subject. Carlyle set to work with enthusiasm, writing the essay which was to be known by the title 'Characteristics'. Carlyle despatched it to Napier not knowing whether it would prove acceptable, and almost not caring, feeling certain that 'the thing has some truth in it, and could find vent elsewhere'. Napier received it 'with respect', yet found it 'inscrutable on first perusal'. Carlyle's own fear was that it might be too 'scrutable'. The essay was published without alteration in December 1831 and Carlyle reported happily that Napier 'seems to be on the best terms with me'.[37]

He might not have been so sanguine if he had seen Napier's postbag. Macaulay claimed that Carlyle might just as well have written in Irving's unknown tongue, and reported that the *Sun* had absurdly attributed the article to Brougham. Jeffrey wrote almost immediately: 'I fear that Carlyle will not do, that is, if you don't take the liberties and the pains with him that I did, but striking out freely, and writing in occasionally.' Carlyle was both obstinate and conceited, and unfortunately had people to abet and applaud him, which was a great pity, 'for he is a man of genius and industry, and with the capacity of being an elegant and impressive writer'.[38]

Napier seemed not unduly concerned, for he accepted Carlyle's offer of a piece on Ebenezer Elliott's *Corn-Law Rhymes*, provided it was popular and not doctrinal. His response to the article, however, was less than enthusiastic. Three weeks' silence followed the receipt of the manuscript, leading Carlyle to 'fancy my radicalism has brought him to a still-stand'.[39] The proofs then followed, with a request for a cut in the article, which Carlyle refused to undertake. The manuscript was published unaltered in July 1832, but by October no payment had been made for either 'Characteristics' or 'Corn-Law Rhymes'. In January 1833 Carlyle still had not been paid for the latter article. This can only have been intended as a deliberate discouragement, for Napier's contributors, apart from Carlyle, regularly praised him for his generous and prompt payments.

As with 'Characteristics', Napier's disenchantment was undoubtedly owing to the reactions of other contributors. MacCulloch wrote in August shortly after publication of the July number: 'Mac and me were clutching our wits the other night to find out what could induce a person of your sound good sense to insert Craigenputtock on Corn.' Rumours he had heard suggested that it would materially damage the Review, and that if Napier got off with the loss of a hundred subscribers it would be very well: 'Craigenputtock is no object of charity — he has a good farm, a handsome wife and a family etc. and if he will not write with some regard to common sense he had better keep his articles for posthumous publication, or print them at his own expense.'[40]

The letter explains much. Carlyle, although still full of ideas for a fourth article, sensed that his association with the *Edinburgh Review* was at an end. Payment for 'Corn-Law Rhymes' was made in March 1833, eight months late, and at a shabbily low rate. A dinner with Napier followed, which went off pleasantly enough, but Carlyle reckoned him 'a dry, faint-hearted wooden kind of man, whom I think I shall not get far with', as he told his mother. Napier 'listens with silence and amazement to my Teufelsdreckism, being himself a solid, old-established Edinburgh Whig,' he told Mill early in 1833.[41]

'Corn-Law Rhymes' was Carlyle's last article for the *Edinburgh*. Napier's recalcitrance undoubtedly soured the relationship, and the cooling of Carlyle's old friendship with Jeffrey further lessened his connection with the Review. Napier's behaviour was uncharacter-istically maladroit and ungenerous. The conclusion must be that he felt that with Macaulay secure and with Brougham to contend with he had not the energy or the inclination to court Carlyle or to take the 'liberties and pains' with him that Jeffrey had advised. And as Carlyle and Jeffrey sensed, Napier was both baffled at Carlyle's 'mystical propensities' and alarmed that he might commit the *Edinburgh* to his radical vision.

As Brougham slipped gradually into the background and a new and statesmanlike Macaulay kept a paternal eye on things, the *Edinburgh Review* approached the 1840s as a solid and responsible organ of public opinion, as Bagehot not altogether facetiously had described it. Napier's last seven years (he died in 1847) were comparatively serene. New reviewers such as Nassau Senior, Richard Monckton Milnes, Abraham Hayward and Herman Merivale created their own coterie, attracted to the *Edinburgh* by its undeniable pre-eminence. Even an old adversary, J. S. Mill, came into the fold in 1840 when the

Westminster Review changed hands, determined, he wrote to Napier 'to gain the ear of the liberal party generally, instead of addressing a mere section of it'.[42]

Napier's death was noted by Henry Cockburn in his Journal with a reflection that could apply to many such editors:

> Without absolute learning or talent in the higher senses, he was intelligent and sensible, well read in morals and metaphysics, very industrious; and he had a good, plain, clear style of composition. The 'Encyclopædia' and the 'Review' connected him with the whole science and literature of the country. No such stream can pass through the soil of a good mind without enriching it by its depositations. The misfortune of the process is that the habit of merely delivering others is apt to impair, or at least to supersede, the power of one's own creation. If Napier had not given his best years to the editing of these works, he would probably have produced something worthy of his own.[43]

As with Jeffrey's departure, speculation on his successor was intense. The job passed, appropriately enough, to Empson, and the seat of operations, with Longman's encouragement, finally moved to London. For the first time in forty-five years, the Review was Edinburgh in name only.

Notes

1. Henry Cockburn, *Life of Lord Jeffrey*, 2 vols (Edinburgh: Adam and Charles Black, 1852), I, 279. John Allen (1771–1843) had been an associate of Jeffrey and the other founders of the *Edinburgh* from the beginning, and remained a reviewer into the 1830s. He became the physician and general companion to Lord Holland and a permanent figure in the social life of Holland House. Because of his wide knowledge of politics and personalities, he was frequently consulted both by Jeffrey and by his successor.

2. William Empson (1791–1852) was a prolific contributor to the *Edinburgh* under Jeffrey and Napier. He succeeded Sir James Mackintosh as professor of English law at the East India College, Haileybury in 1824. He married Jeffrey's daughter in 1838, and succeeded Napier to the editorship of the *Edinburgh* in 1847.

3. G. O. Trevelyan, *Life and Letters of Lord Macaulay*, 2 vols (London: Longmans, Green and Co., 1876) I, 186. Myron F. Brightfield, *John Wilson Croker* (London: Allen & Unwin, 1940), pp.196–7. See also Hazlitt, *Works* XX, pp. 43-6

4. *The Collected Letters of Thomas and Jane Welsh Carlyle*, edited by C. R. Sanders and K. J. Fielding, Duke–Edinburgh edition, 12 vols (Durham, NC: Duke University Press, 1976–85), V, 20 n.4.

5. British Library Add. MSS 34614, ff.125, 156.

6. Carlyle, *Letters*, V, 196 n.1

7. BL Add. MSS 34614, f.178; *The Letters of Thomas Babington* Macaulay, ed. Thomas Pinney, 6 vols (Cambridge: Cambridge University Press, 1974), I, 258.

8. BL Add. MSS 34614, ff.246, 251.

9. See John Clive, *Scotch Reviewers: The Edinburgh Review, 1802–1815* (London: Faber and Faber, 1957), p.26 n.

10. *Selection from the Correspondence of Macvey Napier*, edited by Macvey Napier (London: Macmillan, 1879), p.69.

11. See Robert Stewart, *Henry Brougham 1778–1868: his Public Career* (London: Bodley Head, 1985), pp.249 *et seq.*

12. Macaulay, *Letters*, I, 281, 298–99, 309–11. *Napier*, p.88.

13. Macaulay, *Letters*, I, 313.

14. BL Add. MSS 34615, ff.429, 365.

15. BL Add. MSS 34615, f.195.

16. Trevelyan, I, 67. The separation was not complete, however. John Clive, in *Thomas Babington Macaulay, The Shaping of the Historian* (London: Secker and Warburg, 1973), p.203, notes how the *Edinburgh* articles often reinforced and reflected the major points of Macaulay's speeches.

17. BL Add. MSS 34615, f.89.

18. Quoted by Arthur Aspinall, *Lord Brougham and the Whig Party* (Manchester: Manchester University Press, 1927), p.207.

19. Napier, pp.168, 201, 218, 219, 225–6.

20. BL Add. MSS 34619, ff.66, 76.

21. Macaulay, *Letters*, III, 255.

22. James Stephen's father (1758–1832) had been closely involved in the Wilberforce circle, and his second wife was Wilberforce's sister (see DNB). The younger Stephen was a step-nephew of Wilberforce, and also his executor, and had been consulted regularly throughout the preparation of the book.

23. See the DNB entry for Thomas Clarkson (1760–1832) for details of the controversy.

24. Brougham had had a quarrel with the elder Stephen. 'S. is an enemy & always was, and the review always took Clarkson's side till last Jany. C was a Foxite & is & will die one, and the Review, *unknown to you* by S's vile trick was reduced to the enemy's quarters.' See BL Add. MSS 34619, f.323.

25. BL Add. MSS 34619, f.285.

26. *Napier*, p.208, 218.

27. *Napier*, p.229, Macaulay, *Letters*, III, 250–1.

28. Macaulay, *Letters*, III, 250–1.

29. Macaulay, *Letters*, III, 256–7.
30. Macaulay, *Letters*, I, 314; III, 251; IV, 167.
31. *Napier*, pp.196, 198, 260.
32. Macaulay, *Letters*, III, 257; *Napier*, pp.271–5.
33. Macaulay, *Letters*, III, 243.
34. Macaulay, *Letters*, III, 293; IV, 17–18.
35. David Alec Wilson, *Carlyle to 'The French Revolution' 1826–1837* (London: Kegan Paul, 1924), p.116.
36. Carlyle, *Letters*, V, 195, 297, 310–11. Naso was Carlyle's nickname for Napier, a reference to his prominent nose. See Carlyle, *Letters*, V, 297 n.2.
37. Carlyle, *Letters*, V, 355; VI, 70, 85, 125.
38. Macaulay, *Letters*, II, 113; *Napier*, p.126.
39. Carlyle, *Letters*, VI, 176.
40. BL Add. MSS 34615, f.382.
41. Carlyle, *Letters*, VI, 311, 301.
42. *The Earlier Letters of John Stuart Mill*, ed. Francis E. Mineka, *The Collected Works of John Stuart Mill*, (London: Routledge, 1963), XIII, 430.
43. *Journal of Henry Cockburn 1831–1854*, 2 vols (Edinburgh: Edmonston and Douglas, 1874), II, 167–8.

Chapter 3

LOCKHART, CROKER AND THE *QUARTERLY REVIEW*

William Gifford, the first editor of the *Quarterly*, had been dogged by ill health through most of his editorship, but this had worsened in 1823. John Wilson Croker and John Barrow, two of the Review's stalwarts, had agreed to assist Gifford through to the sixtieth number, due out in January 1824. John Murray, the publisher, was aware that the selection of a successor was urgent, but he hung back in the hope that once again Gifford would rally and the decision could be deferred.

Walter Scott tentatively proposed that Southey, one of the most prolific of the regular reviewers, be persuaded to take over, a proposal acceptable neither to Gifford nor to Murray, as Southey knew: 'I am considered by Murray as too bigoted and by Gifford as too liberal,' he wrote to a friend. Southey in turn pressed the case of John Taylor Coleridge,[1] nephew of the poet and a rising young barrister with literary inclinations as well as an occasional reviewer. Murray made an overture to Coleridge in 1823 but then cautioned him against letting the proposed editorship influence his other plans. Irritated by Murray's vacillation, Southey feared that Coleridge might be damaged by being considered as his personal candidate. He also thought Murray was bent on putting the management of the *Quarterly* more closely under his own control. Both suspicions were in part correct.[2]

Finally, in December 1824 the offer of the editorship was formally made to Coleridge. The terms of the agreement, Coleridge's view of the matter and his commitment to the *Quarterly* are unclear. Some of his friends considered it imprudent of him to undertake any activity which might possibly interrupt his steady rise in the legal profession. In retrospect it was generally assumed that he had taken the editorship temporarily. Whatever the circumstances, it was to be an extremely short tenure.

Murray's attentions were elsewhere in the late summer of 1825. He had caught the ear of the 20-year-old Benjamin Disraeli, the son of his old friend and confidant, Isaac d'Israeli,[3] who had become a reader and an unofficial assistant in the firm while also involving himself in some speculations in Mexican mining ventures. Murray was keen to establish a Tory daily newspaper which would rival *The Times* and which would have a more regular and immediate impact on public affairs than the less frequent *Quarterly*.[4] The scheme was hatched, with Disraeli's encouragement, in the spring and summer of 1825, with half the funds to be raised by Murray and the remaining half by Disraeli and J. D. Powles, an associate in his mining ventures.[5]

The most pressing need was for an editor, not an obviously attractive post in a period when the political significance of the newspaper press was becoming recognized, but when intellectually and socially, it was still associated either with scurrility or flagrant commercial partisanship. Armed with letters of introduction, Disraeli was dispatched to Scotland to woo John Gibson Lockhart, now the son-in-law of Sir Walter Scott and known to Murray from his connections with *Blackwood's Magazine* and through Scott's connections with the *Quarterly*.[6]

Lockhart at this period had acquired a not altogether enviable reputation as a *Blackwood's* contributor and as a novelist of modest talents. He had been nicknamed 'the Scorpion' in an anonymous pamphlet, and the epithet had stuck. His *Blackwood* activities had been the subject of a further attack by John Scott, the editor of the *London Magazine*, in 1820, for which he had demanded an apology or satisfaction. In the duel that followed his place had been taken by his friend John Christie, who fatally wounded Scott. Although he was the injured party and technically innocent, the affair permanently scarred Lockhart's reputation.[7] By any standard, he was a somewhat risky choice for the editor of a newspaper.

The conjunction of the outrageously dandified, confident,

engaging Disraeli and the cool, stiff, cautiously self-regarding Lockhart was surprisingly successful in personal terms. Disraeli spent a fortnight at Chiefswood, Lockhart's home, in September and persuaded Lockhart to make a return visit to London in early October. In professional terms, however, the expedition faltered. Neither Scott nor Lockhart was prepared to sacrifice Lockhart's professional reputation in Scotland, however tarnished, and his prospects at the bar, for the precarious and socially less desirable position of newspaper editor. Disraeli did his best to aggrandize the position by making it purposely vague. Lockhart would be coming to London, not as the editor of a newspaper, but as 'Director-General of an immense organ and at the head of a band of high-bred gentlemen and important interests'. The salary mentioned was large, although neither Lockhart nor Scott regarded it as excessive, and there was talk too of finding Lockhart a seat in Parliament and a place at the English bar. But the obstacle that remained, as Disraeli reported to Murray, was the 'losing caste in society' by the association with a newspaper.[8]

The next stage in the negotiations is less clear. It would appear that in the course of Lockhart's visit to London in October, Murray impulsively threw in the offer of the editorship of the *Quarterly*, with the proviso that Lockhart agreed also to an association with the newspaper, writing for it and accepting either a salary or a share in it. According to William Wright, Murray's legal adviser and confidant, Murray had expressed dissatisfaction with Coleridge at this time, and he, Wright, had suggested Lockhart as a replacement, a proposal which Murray eagerly accepted. Whatever its source, the offer of the *Quarterly* editorship was made on the spur of the moment, for Scott only learned of it in mid-October through a letter from Lockhart to his wife Sophia, and then in a letter from Murray, written on 13 October. Murray's choice of Lockhart is the more puzzling because of the severance of his own connection with *Blackwood*'s in 1819, having been its London publisher and joint proprietor, because of his dislike of the play of personality in the magazine, a feature for which Lockhart as well as John Wilson and James Hogg were generally held responsible.

Events moved swiftly. Two agreements, dated 20 October 1825, stipulated that Lockhart would receive £1,200 per annum as editor of the *Quarterly*, with the possibility of earning more by his own contributions, plus a fee of £1,500 per annum for his work for the newspaper, with the option of exchanging the latter salary for a one-eighth share in the paper.[9] Lockhart and Scott professed themselves satisfied, in terms of both status and finance, and Lockhart prepared to remove his family to London.

Murray appeared to have acted without consultation. Coleridge was not told of the appointment of a successor until the day before the announcement appeared in *The Times*. Nor were any of the *Quarterly*'s regular contributors informed of the change. William Stewart Rose, a friend of both Murray and Scott and a long-time *Quarterly* supporter, was first to raise the alarm by reporting the news to John Barrow, who went immediately to Murray to protest. Successive ripples of protest soon involved a larger circle. The furore focused on Lockhart's literary past, more specifically the *Blackwood* connection and the repercussions of the Scott–Christie duel.

The ground swell soon reached Murray, who by this time was alarmed by his own temerity and sent Disraeli back to Scotland to persuade a puzzled Scott to write round to various of the protestors in support of his son-in-law and in particular to set minds at rest with regard to the cessation of Lockhart's connection with *Blackwood's*. Scott's reply to Murray was a model of loyalty, arguing that the follies of a youth of twenty-three or four should not be held against a man of thirty, adding that he had insisted that Lockhart abandon his satirical activities when he asked for the hand of Sophia Scott. He also emphasized Lockhart's scholarly qualities and his willingness to seek advice. In his own mind he was less sure of the present state of the *Blackwood* connection and of how far Lockhart had been lured back 'among the Ambrosians'.

He was right to be nervous, for Lockhart had indeed kept up his links. As late as August 1824 he was writing a part of the 'Noctes Ambrosianae' at Croker's behest, and also contributing to the 'Letters of Timothy Tickler'.[10] Scott's letter to Southey, written at Murray's insistence, took pains to emphasize that the proposal of the *Quarterly* editorship had come out of the blue, and that he had had no part in initiating it or in the unseating of Coleridge. Southey's reply absolved Scott of any blame, and professed measured support for Lockhart, despite the *Blackwood* factor. His ire was reserved for Murray's handling of the affair, and in particular his treatment of Coleridge, to whose cause he remained loyal.[11]

Little of the disquiet seems to have centred on the incumbent editor's predicament. Scott was worried that Lockhart's visit to London would appear to have hastened Coleridge's dismissal. A comment from Lord Gifford, an English law lord, to the effect that Coleridge would be best advised to give up the Review as it would prevent his progress in the legal profession, supported the general view that Coleridge had already begun to find the combination of legal and editorial work onerous.

Even if this were the case, Murray's procrastination in informing him of Lockhart's appointment was extremely insensitive. Southey confirmed that Coleridge regarded the whole thing as 'a deliverance' but was incensed that neither he nor Coleridge had been informed before the announcement in *The Times* for 17 November. Disraeli reported to Lockhart on 21 November that Murray had by then spoken to Coleridge, that nothing could have gone off better and that the whole affair was now perfectly settled. Testimonies to the handsomeness of Coleridge's behaviour were accorded on all sides, and equally to Murray's bad handling of the affair. 'It is plain the Emperor of the West like other potentates was at first too precipitate and sanguine, and then like MacBeth was afraid to look on what he had done,' Scott commented to Lockhart.[12]

The position of the outgoing editor, however, attracted little sympathy. There was far too much emotion surrounding the appointment of his successor. Scott's letter of 17 November had pacified Murray, and Disraeli predicted that his eyes would soon be opened to 'the junta of official scamps who have too long enslaved you', meaning, presumably the Admiralty connection of Barrow and Croker.[13] Lockhart had written to Croker, Rose, and George Ellis, another *Quarterly* supporter, as well as to Murray, declaring his virtual severance from *Blackwood's*, which was an interesting gloss on the truth.

Croker's role in Lockhart's appointment at this point had been minimal. Coleridge had written to him in mid-November asking for his support and he had chosen not to answer, preferring, as he later told Lockhart, to keep out of the affair. His relations with both Scott and Lockhart had been cordial for many years. The youthful Lockhart had been associated with *The Constitution*, renamed *The Guardian*, a short-lived attempt by Croker to establish a Tory newspaper in 1819–20. Croker had been a useful and obliging link with influential political circles and his relationship with Scott in particular had been one of affection and respect. Scott certainly saw no reason for Croker to be included among Murray's backroom objectors. 'As for Canning and Croker I take it they would not care sixpence if you had been Kit North from beginning to end — I will swear for the last at any rate,' he wrote confidently to Lockhart at the height of the protests against his appointment.[14]

Certainly Lockhart perceived Croker to be a potential ally, writing to him on 16 November to urge that 'one word from you can dispel the darkest cloud that ever disturbed the serenity of his [Murray's] mind'. Croker replied that he had been kept in the dark as to Lockhart's appointment and that he had chosen not to become involved when Coleridge had asked for his support. He did reveal that some months previously he had heard of Murray's plans for another newspaper and that he had 'knocked it on the head, that is, knocked it out of his', or so he had thought. Lockhart was swift to assure Croker of his surprise that he had not been consulted by Murray over changes to the *Quarterly* or his further plans for a newspaper, adding unctuously, 'I have always, like the rest of the world, considered your own papers as among the most valuable supports.'[15]

Murray's persistence with plans for his newspaper clearly rankled with Croker, possibly because it was he who had induced Murray to become a partner in *The Guardian* in 1820 and he considered himself to be the link man between the Tory party and the newspaper press. Whether this led to further words between them is unclear. Possibly encouraged by Disraeli, Murray's anger and irritation over the opposition to Lockhart were shortly to be focused on Croker rather than on Barrow or Rose.

Disraeli was by this time devoting his full energies to Lockhart's cause, spending three painful hours with Murray on 22 November, assuring him of Lockhart's soundness. Letters of reassurance to Lockhart followed, adding that Murray had not until now 'any conception of the utter worthlessness of the intriguing, selfish and narrowminded officials by whom he has been so long surrounded. The Scales however have at length fallen from our friend's eyes and the walls of the Admiralty have resounded to his firm and bold but gentlemanly tones.'[16]

Lockhart, meanwhile, wrote to Croker, supposedly clearing up the ambiguity of his connection with Murray's projected newspaper, confessing that he had agreed to become 'to a trifling extent, of course, a proprietor of this paper should it really be established', adding that the business having gone on without Croker's sanction, 'throws, in my eyes, a considerable cloud over it'. As further concilation he cautioned Croker not to find Murray's conduct wavering and inconsistent: 'you and he have never rightly understood each other'.[17]

Murray then wrote to Lockhart declaring that, as a result of his discussions with Disraeli, 'heaven and Earth may pass away but it cannot shake my opinion and I am prepared to go on with you with every good feeling and every exertion of which my nature is capable'. Lockhart's plans for the Review were 'noble and just' but those for the newspaper were 'magnificent and very far beyond my previous conception', an interesting contrast with Lockhart's disclaimer to Croker as to the insignificance of his involvement with the paper. A second letter to Lockhart the following day spoke ominously of 'the deceitful conduct of a certain individual', who would 'avail himself of any means in his power to divert you from our purpose'.[18]

On Murray's part it was clearly a case of the rubbing of an old wound. Croker had had no hand in the opposition to Lockhart, despite popular assumptions to the contrary. Indeed he had known nothing of the appointment until the protest mounted by Barrow and Rose was well under way. The quarrel between Murray and Croker, rekindled by the *Quarterly*'s editorial crisis, was over Murray's newspaper activities, not his choice of editor.

Sensing that the wind had changed, Lockhart promptly did an astonishing about turn. Croker's behaviour had distressed him, he told Murray. He had had no idea that the feelings between Murray and Croker were other than friendly. It was clearly 'now over with us for the present'. But he did not regard it as an event of much moment: 'On the contrary, I believe that his papers in the Review have (with a few exceptions) done the work a good deal more harm than good.' They contained 'the bitterness of Gifford without his dignity, and the bigotry of Southey without his *bonne-foi*.' Provided they could obtain the same information elsewhere, they need not regret 'the secretary's quill'. He encouraged Murray to have a a quiet word with both Barrow and Rose, who could, he predicted, easily be persuaded that their fears were groundless.[19]

Thus the outcome of the move against Lockhart was quite unlike what might have been anticipated. The 'secretary's quill' was virtually absent for the next five years, which fuelled the speculation that it had been Croker who initially launched the objections to Lockhart, a speculation which anyone familiar with their association from 1819 onward would have found difficult to sustain.[20] Croker's withdrawal coincided with a period of intense political activity, the advent of the Duke of Wellington's government, the passing of the Catholic Emancipation Bill, and the prelude to the Reform Bill — a period when not only Croker's pen, but his advice and his contacts, would have been extremely useful.

Lockhart's toadyism to Murray, coupled with the abrogation of friendship with Croker, a *volte face* accomplished within a matter of days once he had sensed the direction in which events were moving, presents him in an extremely unattractive light. The contrast between Lockhart's letter to Croker on 21 November with that to Murray on 27 November is breathtaking, as is his blurring of the truth about his connections both with Murray's newspaper and with *Blackwood's*. Having accepted Murray's offer of the *Quarterly* editorship on the spur of the moment, a decision with profound implications both personally and in terms of his career, and with the undesirable connection with a newspaper still preying on his mind, Lockhart was clearly shaken by the opposition to his appointment. The speed of his response to Murray's letter, the flattery and the immediate dropping of Croker were the result of insecurity and near panic.

To be fair, all of the personalities involved in the affair were complex, Murray's no less than the others. Disraeli, Croker and Lockhart independently testified to his vacillation and weakness. Byron's memorable phrase, 'the most timorous of God's booksellers', was evoked by everyone associated with the incident in turn. Scott pronounced him 'though a good fellow... in point of steadiness a reed shaken with the wind' and Rose declared him 'all sail & no ballast & upon whom one puff tells as well as another'. Croker ventured that 'like other weak people, he *commits* himself on such or such a point & then goes round the circle of his acquaintance until he can find someone whose advice may countenance the source to which he had already pledged himself'. Murray's own admission that he had been dilatory about informing Coleridge of Lockhart's appointment because of a dislike of unpleasant tasks was a rare display of self-knowledge. Lockhart felt it necesary to add, in his letter of 27 November, denouncing Croker: 'To all these people — Croker as well as the rest — John Murray is of much more importance than they can ever be to him if he will only *believe* what I know viz. that his own name in *society* stands miles above any of theirs'. It was a surprising comment from one so junior and so recently brought into Murray's orbit — but it suggests that the writer knew his man. The fact that the 20-year-old Disraeli could so easily work himself into the confidence and trust of his father's old friend as to become the driving force behind the projected newspaper was another sign of the publisher's susceptibility to influence. Murray himself spoke of 'yielding' to Disraeli's 'unrelenting excitement and importunity'.[21]

Plans for the paper, which Disraeli named *The Representative*, chugged on, with the appointment of William Maginn as Paris correspondent and other contributors notionally distributed in foreign centres, as well as arrangements for a London office. But the collapse of a South American mining venture and the general financial panic at the end of 1825 resulted in the withdrawal of two of the paper's main financial backers, Disraeli and his colleague J. D. Powles, who together had been responsible for half of the capital for the paper. Disraeli's association with the project came to an abrupt end.[22]

The exact nature of the breach between Disraeli and Murray is unknown. Blake, Disraeli's biographer, suggests that there might have been factors other than financial which produced the rift. Murray subsequently spoke of 'untruths' told him by Disraeli and of aspects of the latter's conduct during the planning of the paper, which he had discovered subsequently. Whatever the reason, it is clear that Disraeli's connection with the newspaper ceased in December 1825, and despite later allegations he had no involvement in the running of the paper.[23]

Disraeli was by this time busy with his first novel, *Vivian Grey*, which was to present a bizarre finale to his association with Murray, *The Representative* and the *Quarterly* circle. Written in the early months of 1826 and published in April, the autobiographical novel in the silver fork mould drew heavily on Disraeli's involvement with Murray, Lockhart and the newspaper, translating the plot from the world of journalism to the world of politics. Other than this, no attempt was made to disguise the characters, and Lockhart as Cleveland and Murray as the Marquess of Carabas were generally recognized. The novel included a scene at the Marquess's dining table where his drunkenness was explicit. The furore surrounding the novel's publication coincided with the period of the failing *Representative* and must have compounded Murray's bitterness and his sense of a breach of trust.[24]

The publication of *Vivian Grey* led to a break between Murray and Disraeli and between Murray and Isaac d'Israeli which was never completely healed. Letters flew back and forth between Murray and all three members of the d'Israeli family, including Mrs d'Israeli, but although civility was restored, and although Murray published two of Disraeli's books in the 1830s, the old warmth and intimacy never returned. Disraeli became a *bête noir* to Murray and his circle. As Blake pointed out, in the 1820s and 1830s they were a powerful set of enemies to acquire. Disraeli was virtually excluded from the

Quarterly for the next twenty years, despite attempts to have his novels reviewed. He was refused admission to the Athenaeum, and attributed the snub to Croker. His unmistakable portrait of Croker as Rigby, the politically ambitious toady of Lord Monmouth and writer of 'slashing' articles in a political review in *Coningsby* (1844) was a way of getting his own back but he must have more than once regretted the youthful precosity and rashness which had produced *Vivian Grey*.[25]

Lockhart now set himself the task of building a reputation in the London literary world. Throughout the protests over his appointment to the *Quarterly* Scott had been supportive, arguing that one or two solid numbers of the Review would do more to quieten jitters about Lockhart's suitability for the editorship than any number of letters. But having decided in his own mind that the editorship of the *Quarterly* was commensurate with Lockhart's social standing and his professional expectations, Scott was tireless in his exertions on behalf of both Lockhart and Sophia. Various aristocratic connections were written to to secure their entry into society, sufficient, as he assured Lockhart, for as good a backing as was needed for folks 'who do not wish above a *genteel Competence* of the great world.'[26]

More important were connections with the world of politics and affairs generally. Here Scott feared that Lockhart's past and his manner generally would work against him. There could be no blotting out of the *Blackwood* connections nor in his heart was Scott absolutely sure that the connection had altogether ceased. In public he urged that Lockhart's youthful indiscretions should not be held against him, and in private he entreated that he should eschew his old acquaintances and resist the temptation to 'drop into the *gown and slipper* garb of life and live with funny easy companions'. Lockhart's much commented upon reserve, his coldness and what Scott termed his 'Hidalgo' air (an Hidalgo was a minor Spanish grandee — the reference was in part to Lockhart's appearance and in part to his manner) had not endeared him to Edinburgh society. Scott thought these would be less of a disadvantage in London where genius and sheer ability would usually triumph over mere mannerisms. To his friends Scott continued to sing Lockhart's praises, reassuring Southey that when he got to know him he would realize that his offer of continued support for the Review was more than justified, and telling another friend that in his view Lockhart was probably 'the best calculated of any man I know' to discharge 'this great critical task'. Dining with Peel, Lord Liverpool and the Duke of Wellington at Croker's invitation in 1826 Scott ruefully confided to his Journal that he wished he could turn a little of his own popularity with 'these magnificoes' to the advantage of Lockhart 'who cannot bustle for himself'.[27]

The English bar and a Parliamentary seat had been mentioned more than once in the negotiations leading up to Lockhart's removal to London. Scott was sceptical on both counts, particularly since Lockhart's poor speaking ability had largely contributed to his mediocre performance at the bar in Scotland. Advice from England also suggested that literature and the law were not such compatible careers as was fondly believed to be the case in Scotland. In any event the bar soon faded as a serious prospect, once Lockhart became enmeshed in the *Quarterly* and other commitments with Murray.

A seat in Parliament held more attractions, particularly with the political voice of the *Quarterly* in mind. Lockhart told Murray early in 1826 that he was expecting to be adopted for an Essex constituency, and as late as March 1831 informed him that he was hoping to become an MP. Whatever tentative offers may have been made, nothing seems to have come of them. According to Andrew Lang, Lockhart's biographer, it was Scott who eventually dissuaded him from pursuing a Parliamentary career on the grounds of his poor public speaking.

The problem of political contacts remained. Scott and others, notably William Wright, were of the opinion that Canning had been instrumental in promoting Lockhart's cause with regard to the *Quarterly* editorship. A certain amount of political contact seemed thus assured, an assurance which was quickly shattered in February 1827 when Canning wrote to Scott in response to a request for a small sinecure for Lockhart, 'a place in the Excise', which had been brought to Scott's attention by Sophia Lockhart. Lockhart had the reputation in London, Canning told Scott, of having been invited from Scotland to be at the head of an anti-Government and particularly an anti-Canning press. A stunned Scott took steps immediately to correct this unfortunate misconception, and Canning pronounced himself fully satisfied. Nothing tangible issued from this, however, and Canning's death later in 1827 left Scott taking his suit to the Duke of Wellington. The one time when Lockhart might have ingratiated himself, when asked by the Duke through Croker to assist with a new Tory evening newspaper, he declined, influenced in part by concern for his own skin, his continued distaste for newspaper writing and more significantly, because he was irritated that the approach had been made through Croker and not directly to himself.[28]

Despite the furore surrounding his appointment Lockhart had begun almost at once to think himself into the *Quarterly*. Early in November, even before the protests had gained a head, he began to plan articles for his first number and asked Murray to send him as many recent Parliamentary reports and official documents as possible, presumably to prepare himself for both the *Quarterly* and his involvement with *The Representative*. He was horrified, he told John Wilson, by the quality of the articles in stock, 'not worth five shillings', and concluded that Coleridge had been living on the stock bequeathed by Gifford and 'the contributions of a set of d——d idiots of Oriel'.[29]

His relationship with Murray was cordial. With characteristic generosity the publisher had offered Lockhart and his family accommodation at his home in Whitehall Place and later insisted on contributing to the rent for Sussex Place, Lockhart's eventual London base.

For the first six months of 1826 Murray was preoccupied by the affairs of *The Representative* which from the beginning had spelled disaster. Lockhart reported that Murray behaved 'like an idiot', changing his mind daily on the paper's political policy, cancelling his own orders, and drinking heavily in the evenings, thus incapacitating himself for serious business.[30] The absence of a firm editor, the haphazard organization of correspondents and the paper's dull style hastened its demise. In July, six months after its launch, the paper ceased publication, loosing Murray an estimated £26,000. Lockhart kept his distance, despite the contract signed in conjunction with the *Quarterly* contract, and felt curiously guilty that he had been at all implicated in the business, while at the same time assuring Murray that the whole affair had proved to him that he had not 'the iron nerves of the man fitted for daily collision with the world'.[31]

On the *Quarterly* front the atmosphere was more serene. With Murray, Lockhart was deferential, eager to learn, and quick to point out his lack of familiarity with both the London literary scene and the larger political world. He called diplomatically on Gifford, as if to emphasize the line of succession.[32] As had been the case with Gifford,

Murray was quick to involve Lockhart in his general publishing activities, which were intricately bound up with the affairs of the *Quarterly*, and Lockhart was soon commenting on new proposals, work in hand, and on the suitability of a work for inclusion in the Family Library or another of Murray's series.

Murray in many respects was his own editor, a situation which it suited Lockhart to encourage. Lockhart was tentative in his suggestions, deferred to his judgement, made diplomatic reference to 'your Review' and assumed that the final decisions were his. It was often Murray who decided which articles should begin or end the number, for how long the Review could be held up for a last minute political paper, and at which point a number was to be sent off to the printer, all essentially editorial matters. In the early days articles and suggestions for articles were sent firstly to Murray who then passed them on to Lockhart for comment. Even in the mid-1830s, when Lockhart had been in the post for nearly ten years, and Murray's son, John Murray III, had begun to give some assistance with the Review, both he and Lockhart had a tendency, on occasion, to behave like timorous editorial assistants, anxious not to overstep their authority. And yet, the situation was remarkably free of tensions. Only once, in 1828, was there any hint of irritation or defiance on Lockhart's part, when he wrote to Murray to 'insist on your not further coming between me & what I consider an essential part of my duties', and even that situation seems to have been quickly smoothed over.[33]

The friendship of Croker and Lockhart, which stemmed from the latter's involvement with *The Constitution* in 1819–20, was affected but not destroyed by the fracas over the editorship. Correspondence between them continued, although it was noticeably sparser and more formal. Scott was a useful link. Croker maintained his affection and concern for his old colleague, particularly in the light of Scott's recent financial difficulties, often commmunicating with him through Lockhart. Even a public dispute between Scott and Croker in 1826 over a threat to Scottish currency, resulting in Scott's 'Letters from Malachi Malgrowther' and Croker's reply in *The Courier* failed to damage the relationship and early in 1827 Scott was predicting that Croker could be lured back into active service.[34]

But a serious breach had occurred between Croker and Murray, whatever the cause, and it left the *Quarterly* without a direct line to government sources at a time when these were vital. The loss was entirely the Review's. Croker was scarcely affected by the situation. Politically it was a volatile period, with Canning's death in 1827, the formation of Goderich's fragile ministry, followed by that of the Duke of Wellington in 1828. Croker was extremely active on the political front and had plenty to occupy him in his spare moments with the completion of his edition of Boswell's *Life of Johnson* on which he had been engaged for some time. Lockhart noted enviously that Canning and Croker were 'inseparable' in the spring of 1827 but, apart from the sorting out of the misunderstanding as regards Lockhart's own position with Canning, there was no tangible benefit to the *Quarterly*.

Lockhart tried somewhat timidly to bring the *Quarterly* to the attention of the Duke of Wellington, sending him a paper on foreign politics in May 1828, which met with approval although the Duke claimed to want to take issue on particular points and promised to send for Lockhart. A letter from the Duke to Lord Aberdeen apropos of French affairs noted Lockhart to be 'very capable'. A tactful inquiry as to the suitability of a forthcoming article on the currency question the following December produced a tardy and unfavourable response. Lockhart had become jittery and irritated by the delay and tried to cancel the article at the last minute, hoping thereby to impress the Duke with his influence over the Review. This proved impossible, so that he was left with the publication of the article shortly after the Prime Minister had voiced his disapproval. Lockhart longed, he told Murray, for a chance to talk these matters over with Croker but he was otherwise engaged.[35]

Croker's absence from the inner counsels had already led to an irrevocable step which was to alienate the *Quarterly* from the government even further. Catholic Emancipation was in the air, and in the summer of 1828 Lockhart expressed the view to Murray that the question would be carried 'in our time', and that the *Quarterly*'s strategy on the issue was clearly a matter of considerable delicacy. Barrow had already offered a pro-Emancipation paper. Croker was known to be in favour as was Scott. Traditionally the *Quarterly* had been pro-Church and anti-Catholic, and as early as December 1825 Southey had urged Lockhart to speak out on the Catholic Question. He continued to press his case, which Lockhart proved unable or unwilling to resist. To the general consternation of one segment of the *Quarterly*'s supporters, the article, which Scott termed 'Southey's great mortar', was fired in the October 1828 issue. Entitled 'The Roman Catholic Question — Ireland' it put the traditional anti-Catholic case with new passion and conviction.[36]

By February 1829 it was public knowledge that the Duke intended to press ahead with Emancipation and the *Quarterly* was seen to have set its course directly in opposition, and wilfully to have aligned itself with the 'old' Tories, a policy that was against Lockhart's better instincts and certainly those of Scott and Croker. It was clear almost immediately that the article was regarded as ill-judged. This was borne out by the fact that it was not separately reprinted, despite Southey's urging. 'Your secession left me to my own poor lights,' Lockhart confessed to Croker much later on; 'I did not then understand the nature of official men at all — as I still do very imperfectly — and had you been by us at the decisive moment to interpret the talk of Downing St. in the dialect of Albemarle St. neither Murray nor I wd. have allowed Southey to tower over us.' The chances of personal preferment and, more important, of a close working relationship between Wellington's government and the *Quarterly*, had virtually been thrown away. The Review would now be forced to choose, Lockhart told Murray the following summer, between the side of the Duke, 'which gives us no information & no substantial support', and that of the old Tories, 'who wd. at least be steady & hearty friends & to whose body, if we have lost Barrow, every one of the writers worth naming is thoroughly attached'.[37]

It was a dilemma which resolved itself. The fall of Wellington's government at the end of November 1830 and the formation of the Grey ministry brought with it Croker's resignation as Secretary of the Admiralty after twenty-two years. The resignation was not obligatory but he chose this time to make what had been a long considered decision. Privately he had also resolved to quit active politics in the event of the Tories being asked to form a ministry in the near future. For the present, though, his Parliamentary activities had never been greater, as the prelude to the Reform Bill began. But the release of his time from the Admiralty meant energies for other things. The rift with Murray had been healing and the process of consultation between Croker, Lockhart and Murray gently resumed from the end of 1828 as messages were passed, views sounded and contributors contacted through Croker. By 1831 he was back in harness with an article in the January issue on 'Military Events in the late French Revolution' and a characteristic political article, 'Friendly Advice to the Lords' (July 1831). This article, Lockhart told Murray, was more admired than anything they had had on politics for years.[38]

Croker now threw himself into the Review with his old vigour. An agreement with Murray made in September 1832 contracted him to produce four sheets of work per number, an average of two articles, for a fee of £150 per number. He reckoned, he told Murray, to have contributed a total of a hundred articles to the first hundred numbers of the Review, to July 1834, and that in the last ten numbers, from December 1832 to April 1835, he had written approximately thirty-four articles.[39]

His parliamentary responsibilities at this time were ferocious in their demands on his time and nervous energy, and he found himself in the House night after night. He was also extremely active behind the scenes as the upper reaches of the Tory party attempted to pull itself together in the wake of the Whig ascendancy. After years of exposure at the centre of Tory politics the *Quarterly* was a welcome respite, and a much valued means of keeping his hand in. 'It really is my life,' Croker told Murray in 1835; 'I should stagnate without it.'[40]

His contributions to the Review had never been exclusively political nor did they become so now. He was constantly at pains to point out that he should not be regarded only as a political reviewer. In practice his tastes were omniverous, from historical works through memoirs, fiction, poetry and travel to the inevitable political articles both domestic and foreign. He was the professional reviewer *par excellence*, virtually inexhaustible in his energies and boundless in his enthusiasm. He was also mercurial, easily riled, capable of blind prejudice, stubborn and often spoiling for a fight — which made him at his best a whimsical, highly entertaining and polished reviewer, and at his worst, like Macaulay, something of a liability.

What it did not do, contrary to the popular impression, was to make him a difficult colleague. From 1831 onwards his relationship with Lockhart was remarkably congenial. The warmth of their old association was renewed. They gradually resumed their former relationship, that of colleagues with mutual interests and a string of common acquaintances, and that relationship deepened over the years. They were tolerant of one another's foibles and able to deal with one another's temperaments. They also complemented one another to the benefit of the Review. Lockhart's lament in the wake of the Catholic Emancipation blunder, that he only imperfectly understood the nature of official men was true. Croker similarly claimed never to have been at home in literary circles: 'My life has been spent between high politics & the most retired domesticity — I never was in literary society & have fewer literary acquaintances or associations than anyone would believe', he told Lockhart at one point. In the *Quarterly* they were, as Croker once said 'like two fingers of the same hand'.[41] It was never the case, as was often thought, that Croker dominated the political policy of the Review to the exclusion of Lockhart, who limply presided over its literary or non-political aspect.

It was a remarkably successful partnership. Lockhart, with increasing tact and expertise, 'managed' Croker. Subjects and books were suggested to him in response to his constant demand for a mixed rather than an exclusively political diet. Lockhart then nudged him tactfully to take a particular line on a book, or to steer a review in a particular direction. He tirelessly sent him newspaper clippings, pamphlets and even appropriate quotations for his reviews, all of which were gratefully and gracefully acknowledged. He smoothed Croker's path in countless other ways, passing on news and gossip, obtaining permission to quote from particular sources and locating obscure editions and other background materials for his articles. The myth of Albemarle St. as the scene of plots and counterplots and internal tensions is not borne out by the evidence. Behind the scenes at the *Edinburgh* was fraught with tension, particularly as Brougham's later influence made itself felt, but the same was not true of the *Quarterly*.

Politically Croker was given a free hand. An article on the current session of Parliament or on a sensitive current issue would be 'welcome' if he chose to do it. The number could be held up for a few days or even a week to suit his convenience if he wished to tackle a current topic, provided the ultimate publication date would not render the article irrelevant. There was never any onus on Croker to do a political article, nor, apart from one instance in 1841, when certain minor alterations were made to ensure consistency with previous policy, was there any substantial editorial interference. Lockhart's editorial activity was exerted at the planning stage, and here, discreetly, he was able to curb Croker's wilder enthusiasm and to moderate the line of argument. The ongoing debate with Macaulay (see Chapter 6) was a case in point.

Lockhart and Croker rarely quarrelled. Once, when a portion of one of Croker's articles was inadvertently altered, Lockhart was abject in his apologies and the matter was dropped. On another occasion, when a deletion made by Croker was accidentally inserted, a profuse apology ensued, and the matter again was dropped. Croker was fourteen years Lockhart's senior, and while at the beginning of their acquaintance this was a major factor, by the mid-1830s it mattered much less. There may have been an element of deference initially, when Croker resumed his role in the *Quarterly*, but there is no suggestion, in any of the vast correspondence between them, that Croker was domineering, that Lockhart cowered under the stronger personality, or that Croker went over Lockhart's head to Murray.

One of the aspects of their long professional relationship was the increasing personal element, which began with the death of Lockhart's son in 1831 and obviously touched a chord in Croker, the death of whose own son in 1820 had been a grievous blow. The death of Scott in 1832 followed by the death of Sophia Lockhart in 1837 increased Croker's personal warmth and sympathy towards Lockhart. Increasingly he became the latter's confidant as ill health, worry, despair over his children and general weariness dogged Lockhart's late middle age. There is a touching letter from Lockhart to Croker in August 1844 taking him into his confidence over an unsuccessful proposal of marriage he made to a Miss Laetitia Mildmay, apparently to the embarrassment of the lady and the consternation of her family.[42]

Rather than an ultimate authority to which either could resort, their mild contempt for Murray was another bond between them. The authority exercised by the publisher on points of procedure, an authority that had been encouraged by Lockhart from the beginning, was in part based on the implicit assumption that his views on important matters were of little consequence. Murray had proved helpful to Lockhart in the summer of 1830 before Croker's return, when Barrow had been difficult and had threatened to withdraw from the Review. Again, when Croker had proved intractable on a particular point, Lockhart asked Murray to write a 'calm' letter to sort out the situation. But there is no other evidence that he acted as a buffer between them, or had any need to do so.

To the contrary, Croker and Lockhart were united in solidarity against Murray's often peremptory behaviour. The July 1837 number contained several surprises in the form of articles Lockhart had not seen. 'You must just bear with this sort of periodical botheration, to which I am getting callous,' he commented to Croker. Murray's mercurial temperament and indecisiveness irritated both his editor and chief contributor. Croker's rueful reflection as early as November 1825, that he doubted whether he or any man could have 'any substantial influence over so unsettled and vacillating a mind', suggested both impatience and the absence of intimacy despite their long standing acquaintance.[43] Feelings between them did not grow much warmer as the years passed.

When, early in 1836 Murray tried to insist that a political article be

done by Sir John Walsh, a Tory MP and political writer whom he
regarded as a valuable acquisition, or failing that, that Croker be
asked to review a pamphlet of Walsh's, with copious extracts, Croker
not only refused, but threatened to withdraw from the Review,
alleging that a 'tone of dictation'[44] had entered an otherwise amicable
agreement. Lockhart worked hard to smooth things over, assuring
Croker of the value Murray placed on his work. Murray in turn
promised not to interfere or to comment on Croker's work. Croker
then assured Murray that he valued his comments and all was well
until the next time. Politeness was the order of the day and on this
occasion it worked. Lockhart assured Croker:

> The stricter your connection with the Q.R. — the larger your
> contributions — the more completely you may take on yourself the
> political department — the more advantageous will it be for the Q.R. ... I
> hope & trust on the whole that the Q.R. is not to lose you. If it does, it
> will go down apace & the Conservative Cause will lose an important
> element of strength & influence.[45]

That the publisher was a burden and a force to be circumvented if
possible was clear. 'Pray forgive all this,' Lockhart wrote after
unburdening himself on one occasion in 1834; 'You know our man &
will understand my ever recurring difficulty with managing him as
well as his review.' 'Murray is in one of his most intractable moods, &
if the eye of the keeper be removed there is no saying what violent
things the maniac may do,' he wrote in October 1839, as his irritation
and disillusion grew. In 1842 he confessed that whereas in the past he
might have been prepared to put up with various annoyances 'out of
pity for the shattered condition Murray had reduced his nerves to', he
was now seriously contemplating retirement. He had been used by
Murray in the past, he hinted, because Murray had assumed that for
financial reasons he was tied to his post.[46]

Murray was clearly not the easiest of proprietors, but it was also
the case that Lockhart's increasing discontent, not just with the
Quarterly but with the course his life had taken generally, made the
relationship more difficult. A stroke suffered in 1841 heralded a
decade of ill health. A much solicited government sinecure, the
auditorship of the Duchy of Lancaster awarded in 1844, removed
some of his financial worries and made retirement a possibility, a
possibility which interestingly he then refused to entertain. Murray,
too, was not well, and died in June 1843. Lockhart's relations with

John Murray III, whom he had known as a boy, were much easier, and with his assumption of the proprietorship, all plans for retirement were shelved. Ironically, Lockhart's commitment to the *Quarterly*, like that of Murray, was to be 'unto death'.[47]

Croker's professionalism and energy as regards his reviewing were remarkable. Political articles often involved consultation with high level contacts on the one hand, and with Lockhart as a sounding board on the other. In contrast, articles on literature of whatever kind, were sheer fun, and Croker's caustic humour, developed in the days of political satire and nurtured during the early years of the *Quarterly*, won him enemies and some surprised and resentful friends. Both he and Lockhart instinctively looked back to the earlier days of political squibs, satire and general debunking which characterized the *Blackwood* era. The pugnacity of their correspondence at times might have seemed self-parody but wasn't. 'I hope you will murder some other Tennyson,' Lockhart wrote after reading Croker's dismissal of the 1833 *Poems*. The poet Lamartine would be 'the better of a good dry rubbing down', he urged for the next number. Hearing on the grapevine that Brougham was said to be worried about a suppressed posthumous attack by Jeremy Bentham, he commented, 'I have sent a Terrier to hunt it out for purposes of plunder'. 'Do favour us with the flagellation of some literary quack,' he suggested on one occasion when a political article was not forthcoming.[48]

At its mildest Croker's style was lightly mocking and generally deflating. Several of his literary reviews became minor *causes célèbres* and attracted the kind of publicity Lockhart could well have done without. Having learned his lesson with the notorious review of Keats's *Endymion* (April 1818), he professed to greater wisdom and improved taste when approaching another new and much heralded poet. The review of Tennyson's 1833 *Poems* (April 1833) was patronizing and generally deflating but hardly murderous. Yet he clearly intended it to establish the *Quarterly* line on the poet. John Sterling's more measured, sympathetic and it must be said, more intelligent review of the 1842 *Poems* (June 1842), provoked a petulant outburst from Croker and a threatened withdrawal from the Review.[49]

The *Quarterly*'s treatment of Harriet Martineau set that writer on a train of revenge against Lockhart and Croker which spilled out in the pages of her autobiography, written in 1855 (it was published posthumously in 1877), and lodged itself permanently in the battery of anti-Croker stories. It also led to a venomous attack on Croker in the *Daily News*, written shortly after his death in 1857, in which she proclaimed him 'the wickedest of reviewers', who 'carried the licence of anonymous criticism to the last extreme', and whose 'foul and false political articles' were 'the disgrace of the periodical literature of our time'.[50]

The attack and the revenge were only partly justified. The *Quarterly*'s first article on her, a review of *Illustrations of Political Economy* (April 1833) was written by G. Poulett Scrope. The second, entitled 'How to observe — Morals and Manners' (June 1839) was by Croker, and the third, a review of her *History of England during the Thirty Years' Peace* (June 1852) was by D. T. Coulton. Scrope's review was fair but critical, arguing that the mixture of fiction and instruction did not work, and that Miss Martineau might do well to look to the work of Maria Edgeworth who was better able to combine fiction with moralizing. Croker's review of *Morals and Manners* was, he would have claimed, full of irony, letting Miss Martineau's 'silliness' speak for itself in a series of extracts accompanied by one or two jibes at her expense and concluding that the work was 'the very foolishest, and most unfeminine farrago we have ever met of apocryphal anecdotes, promiscuous facts, and jumbled ideas, picked at random ... out of the Penny Magazine' (Vol. LXIII, 72). Coulton's review of the *History* which he coupled with Roebuck's *History of the Whig Ministry of 1830*, was highly critical of both fact and interpretation and dissatisfied with the concept of contemporary history.

Coulton's review could not have been mistaken for Croker's work, but the June 1839 'Morals and Manners' review was typical of its author and Miss Martineau clearly believed that both Lockhart and Croker had had a hand in Scrope's April 1833 review as well. The Scrope review was described in her autobiography as a baptism of fire, which tested her powers of endurance to hostile reviews and which did her reputation serious injury. According to her account, Scrope admitted that all aspects of the review which dealt with political economy were his, but that he was 'too much of a gentleman to have stooped to ribaldry or even jest', and that Lockhart and Croker made 'no secret' that the ribaldry was theirs. The original version of the review had been even more offensive, Miss Martineau alleged. Croker had boasted at a dinner party of 'tomahawking Miss Martineau in the *Quarterly*'. The printers had told her that Lockhart had gone down to the office and cut out the worst passages 'at great inconvenience and expense'. There is no hint in any of Croker or Lockhart's correspondence that such interference occurred. The tone of the introductory paragraphs: 'What wonder that, from the Woolsack down to the Penny Cyclopedia, there should be a general chorus of exultation over the Sibylline leaves of Norwich' (Vol. XLIX, 136) and the more aggressive final two pages of the review — 'The best advice we can give her is, to burn all the little books she has as yet written, with one or two exceptions; — to abstain from writing any more till she has mastered a better set of "principles" than the precious stock she has borrowed from her favourite professors' (151) — suggests that they might have been written by another hand, possibly Croker's. His only known comment about her was made in a letter to John Murray III, prior to receiving the revises of the 1839 article. Having heard that Richard Haliburton's *Sam Slick* contained 'some fun' about her, he asked that the book be sent to him, although he felt, he said, that it would probably not offer any additional material 'as she is, herself and by herself, as ridiculous as can be', not the comment, one would think, of a reviewer bent on the lady's destruction.[51]

Nor, in retrospect does the Scrope article appear particularly offensive, and certainly not as devastating as Miss Martineau alleged. Croker's 1839 review could have aroused her anger, and possibly this review coupled with Coulton's in 1852 transformed in retrospect an unwelcome snub to a young writer into a humiliating attack. But in no other respect could Miss Martineau conceivably have been regarded as the hapless victim of Lockhart and Croker's cruel jesting.

Allegations that Croker intervened in certain articles, overruled Lockhart and inserted his own comments, in order to enliven or to stiffen reviews, had currency during certain periods. The one instance of interference which was documented occurred in the same issue as the Scrope review of Harriet Martineau, (April 1833). Philip Henry Stanhope, Lord Mahon, reviewed Lord John Russell's *The Causes of the French Revolution*, a book which no doubt had some interest for Croker with his extensive knowledge of the subject. According to Mahon the review was 'revised' in proof by Croker, the additional material, including some disparaging remarks about Russell, not in accordance with Mahon's view of him. These were most likely to have been the opening three pages, which were more robust in their attack on Russell than the main body of the review, which was generally unfavourable: 'And such trifling, forsooth, is to pass for philosophy and history — for a critical inquiry into the real causes of the French Revolution' (Vol. XLIX, 154). This section picked up Russell on points of language, the kind of detailed carping which Croker enjoyed in his reviewing. The conclusion of the review, which began 'This ridiculous Essay' also suggests itself as a possible Croker interpolation (Vol. XLIX, 174).

When the review appeared Mahon wrote to Murray to protest, declaring that he would never again write for the Review. He made a point of publishing the essay separately, without the 'revisions', in order to make public the degree of interference. Mahon's subsequent account of the affair absolved Lockhart from any blame over the incident, saying that he had understandably preferred the veteran reviewer to the debutante.[52]

Croker viewed the 'Mahonscrape', as he termed it, as an important matter of principle. At stake was the very nature of the bond between the reviewer and the Review, one of the main elements of which was to tell 'no secrets of the printing house', as he told Murray. What had happened to Mahon's article was no more than what any reviewer should expect. All editors had not only the *right* but the *duty* of adding, diminishing or altering articles and any reviewer enlisted in the service of the Review must therefore expect to see alterations and even mutilations. If Murray were to support Mahon, Croker told him, he did not see how either he or Lockhart could continue to remain with the Review.[53]

Resignations did not take place. Murray did agree to publish Mahon's article minus the 'revisions', but his abject apology for this and the argument that he thought it the best way of preventing a scene, conciliated Croker. Lockhart in turn vowed never to permit Mahon to contribute again, a vow which was revoked eight years later in March 1841. The question of Croker's interference remained something of a mystery. That it was more myth than reality has remained the view of Croker's only biographer and erstwhile apologist, Myron F. Brightfield, and of Louis Jennings, the nineteenth-century editor of Croker's letters. Harriet Martineau's account seems overheated and verging on paranoia but the Mahon episode is, on the other hand, fully documented.

What is more difficult to gauge, with hindsight, is the impact of Croker's articles, not just his emendations. His treatment of Fanny

Burney, Madame d'Arblay, on two occasions (April 1833 and June 1842), was ungenerous and unjustifiably waspish. The thrust of his review of her edition of her father's *Memoirs* was that they were more about herself and that the ultimate testimony to her vanity was her careful concealment of her age. *Evelina* was not, as was popularly thought, the work of a mere girl of seventeen, but of a young woman of twenty-five. This ungentlemanly disclosure was to be taken up by Macaulay as an example of Croker's brutish reviewing tactics (see Chapter 6). He sent the review to Lockhart with the comment that it had amused him as he thought it would the readers, 'without any brutality against the poor old body'.[54].

Conceivably he was unaware of the potential impact of the article, as he had been of that on Harriet Martineau. One also suspects him of disingenuousness, on these occasions. In his review of Fanny Burney's *Diary and Letters* nine years later, he returned once again to her 'deception', and guided in part by Lockhart, produced an extremely unsympathetic portrait of her, which contrasted startlingly with Macaulay's more balanced and sympathetic article in the *Edinburgh* six months afterwards (January 1843). The total absence of sympathy and the dogged aggression of the article suggested a personal animus or a vendetta, which has never been satisfactorily explained, although Macaulay claimed it was because she had refused Croker access to some Boswell material in her possession.[55]

Croker adopted a pose of boorishness towards all women writers, coupled with elements of flirtation. Disraeli's portrait of Rigby (see note 25) in this respect hit home: 'it was thought that no one could lash a woman like Rigby'. 'Pray observe how one falls into a discussion of *looks* when a lady author is concerned,' Croker commented to the younger John Murray after being agreeably surprised by Mrs Trollope on their first meeting. Croker was 'desirous to have the rifling of Mrs Frances Butler, d—— her petticoats', Lockhart reported to Murray in the spring of 1835. The first draft of his article on Mrs Butler's (Fanny Kemble) *Journal* (July 1835), which had been published by Murray, made the publisher so nervous he put off reading the proof. Lockhart assured him that Murray thought it 'perhaps the very brightest thing you have done in that line', but was anxious for 'a little softening in the censure, a little heightening of the praise, & another favourable extract'. Croker grudgingly softened a little of the asperity and gave a few more laudable extracts but he resented Murray's using the Review in effect to puff his own publications. He was in general 'wonderfully free from that littleness', Croker told Lockhart.[56]

Much of Croker's critical vocabulary was the legacy of a previous era as was the sardonic tone of his reviews. The aggressiveness and pugnacity, and dismissive tone of much of his reviewing seemed gratuitous and vaguely distasteful, not the wounding or destructive thrusts of an authoritative critic. What is certain, however, is that Croker's activities were not undertaken as a challenge to Lockhart's authority, the actions of a wilful elder statesman who refused to be controlled. They had Lockhart's approval or at least his sanction. Lockhart remained loyal even to the end, when in the late 1840s Croker's increasing irascibility and his distance from the centre of power made him even more of a liability. When a severe review of Sir Francis Head's The *Defenseless State of England* (December 1850) produced a letter to *The Times* Murray tried to use Lockhart to secure Croker's resignation but he refused.[57]

At his peak, Croker was essential to the political survival of the *Quarterly*. His contacts, his experience with the newspaper press and his vast knowledge of the workings of the political world made him irreplaceable. Lockhart was aware of this from an early stage, and aware too that whatever Scott and others could effect by way of introductions, and whatever he could do for himself, he would never satisfactorily fulfil that side of the editor's responsibilities.

But Lockhart did exercise some influence, through Croker, on the political policies of the Review. On several occasions he tactfully steered Croker's articles towards what he considered the right line for the *Quarterly*:

The Q.R. must not be the reflection merely of a few peoples' private views, hopes, or fears. We must I think consider it as bound up in the interests of the Tory party & look *how* without absolutely compromising our own personal consistency, it may be possible for us to serve that cause.

Lockhart was also clear that while serving the Tory party, the *Quarterly* should serve not the Parliamentary party only but the wider constituency:

anything said about politicks in unparliamentary language startles & offends persons used to that language alone — but print is not parliamentary speaking nor does the Q.R. address itself exclusively to great lords & fine gentlemen. It is my opinion that the Q.R. would be incapable of rendering any service to the party if it were to become the mere tool of our chiefs — that it must preserve the attitude of independence & occasionally serve its friends even in spite of themselves.

Again the following year he wrote to Croker:

My opinion is as it always has been that the Q.R. ought to look to the great cause of Conservatism — the defense of our liberties against the tyranny of the democracy embodied in the H. of Commons: & that the interest of the Q.R. is engaged at least as much as its honour in never shrinking from this course under the temptation of any arguments based on mere party expediency.

'There is an essential difference of views between those who have long breathed the atmosphere of St. Stephens — still more of Downing St. — & the Tory mass throughout the country,' Lockhart warned Croker early on; 'For these last, we must I think, have bold words, or they will not be pleased with us.'[58]

The same tact and management that was directed towards literary and general reviewing was exercised in respect of the political articles and the comments and suggestions were rarely resisted. Occasionally Croker was querulous, as in November 1842 when a proposal for an extra number to handle a backlog of articles was floated without consultation. This fuelled his irritation over Sterling's Tennyson article and he wrote to Lockhart to terminate his connection with the Review, reminding him that he was 'now Dean of the Chapter — the only survivor ... of the original set'.[59] But like all the other flareups the matter blew over, and the *Quarterly* went on as usual, if more sluggishly.

By the 1840s Croker, Lockhart and Murray were old men, in spirit if not in years. Murray's death in June 1843 left the other two with an even stronger sense that they were the last of the old guard. John Murray III proved a less temperamental and altogether easier master than his father. Lockhart's relations with him were untroubled. Croker however irritated him by the increasingly erratic nature of his performance. With the fall of Peel and the severance by Croker of thirty-seven years of friendship and political association, his direct line to the centre of Tory politics was cut off and his usefulness to the *Quarterly* drastically curtailed. He became a peripheral figure, opinionated and stubborn and, more often than not, wrong in his approach to political affairs. The editorship was shared by the two old men. Both in failing health they alternated duties according to their fitness.

Lockhart had become weary, disenchanted and resigned to the fact that his professional life would not now take a more interesting turn. The move to London and the *Quarterly* editorship had not proved to be the path to greater glory, as he had hoped. Whether it had been his *Blackwood's* past or the fact of being a transplanted Scot in an English literary scene, or his own particular brand of reserve, which did not lend itself to conviviality of either a social or intellectual sort, Lockhart never became the presence on the London scene that both he and Scott had envisaged as the just deserts of his youthful talents. He was a competent editor at best. In part, he was simply worn down by drudgery.

The nature of the *Quarterly* management, with a prominent publisher and a forceful chief contributor, while not uncongenial, meant that Lockhart was never able to stamp his own mark on the *Quarterly*, to make it, in any sense, his own publication. He was a curiously disappointed man, old before his time, middle-aged in his thirties. He remained as editor until shortly before his death in 1853, but the spark had gone out long before. A comment to Murray in the autumn of 1841 apropos an article he had been trying to encourage from a reluctant contributor, sadly summed up his view of the editor's role:

> I have no *personal* vanity in the least involved. I know very well that the Editor gets no credit at all — Surely I must be an ass if 15 years' experience has not cleared my head of that dream.[60]

Two years later, after Murray's death, he wrote wearily to Croker:

> Time was, when I sighed and prayed for the means of release from the eternal worry of small negotiations & explanations inseparable frm the management of the *Quarterly*. I used to dream of being at liberty to choose my literary tasks, then tasks no longer, for myself — I had fond dreams of doing something permanently worthy in letters. But with life's idle dreams these too have flown. I am persuaded very thoroughly that I am no longer fit for anything better than the course of drudgery which has fallen hitherto to my share & which indeed is probably less disagreeable to me than would have been the pursuing of my old profession at the bar.[61]

It was a sad valedictory.

Notes

In this chapter I have drawn extensively on the correspondence of John Wilson Croker, and in particular on the collection of Croker's papers at the William L. Clements Library of the University of Michigan. A selection of the vast correspondence between John Gibson Lockhart and Croker was edited by the late Professor A. L. Strout and published in *Notes and Queries* between October 1938 and June 1946. I have quoted from this source where appropriate. In addition, selections from the Lockhart–Croker correspondence from the Clements Library and from the Lockhart collection at the National Library of Scotland were edited by students of Professor Strout and presented as MA dissertations at Texas Technological College, now the Texas Technological University, Lubbock, Texas. Where possible I have quoted from these dissertations, the details of which are as follows:

Lott, Woodrow Wilson, 'The Lockhart–Croker Correspondence', Vol. I (1940).
Quanah Lewis, 'The Lockhart–Croker Correspondence', Vol. II (1940).
X.C. Keithley, 'The Lockhart–Croker Correspondence', Vol. III (1940).
Nell M. Wiley, 'The Lockhart–Croker Correspondence', Vol. IV (1941).
Margaret C. Davis, 'Letters of Croker to Lockhart' Vol. I (1947).
Emma B. Reeves, 'Letters of Croker to Lockhart', Vol. II (1949).

I have also made use of the extensive manuscript holdings relating to the *Quarterly Review* in the archives of John Murray Publishers. As this collection is not fully catalogued, I have given the dates of letters where possible.

1. Sir John Taylor Coleridge (1790–1876), judge. After a brilliant undergraduate career, Coleridge was elected to a fellowship at Exeter College, Oxford (1812), and later called to the bar (1819). His family connections and his own inclinations drew him to literary circles, and he contributed sporadically to the *Quarterly*. Prudence, possibly, later suggested that a legal career was the more likely option. Coleridge wrote a *Memoir of Keble* (1869), who had been a close friend since their undergraduate days. See DNB.
2. Samuel Smiles, *A Publisher and his Friends: Memoir and Correspondence of the late John Murray*, 2 vols (London: John Murray, 1891), II, 162, 164; *Familiar Letters of Sir Walter Scott*, 2 vols (Edinburgh: David Douglas, 1894), II, 359, 374n.; *New Letters of Southey*, 2 vols ed. K. Curry (New York: Columbia University Press, 1965), II, 268, 272, 276.
3. Isaac d'Israeli (1766–1848), best known for his collection, *The

Curiosities of Literature, (1791–3, 1823).

4. Murray was constantly beset with offers of involvement with periodical publications, a prospect which was not unattractive. After abandoning his joint proprietorship of *Blackwood's* in 1819, he was offered half the property of the *Daily Sun*, and also a partnership in William Jerdan's *Literary Gazette*, both of which he refused. He was then induced by Croker to become a partner in the short-lived *Guardian* in 1820 and early in 1823 he was offered the *British Review*, which he declined.

5. Powles was principal partner in the firm of J. and A. Powles, a leading firm of South American merchants. See *Benjamin Disraeli Letters, 1815–1834*, ed. J. A. W. Gunn, John Matthews, Donald M. Schurman and M.G. Wiebe, 2 vols (Toronto; University of Toronto Press, 1982), I, 24n.

6. Southey, *New Letters*, II, 292, claimed that he had asked Croker to be editor and when Croker had 'laughed at him' had gone in search of Lockhart. There is no supporting evidence for this claim.

7. See Andrew Lang, *The Life and Letters of John Gibson Lockhart*, 2 vols (London: John C. Nimmo, 1897), I, 236–92 for a full account of the affair.

8. *The Letters of Sir Walter Scott*, ed. H. J. C. Grierson, Centenary Edition, 12 vols (London: Constable, 1932), IX, 249–50; Disraeli, *Letters*, I, 38–9. Smiles, II, 191–2.

9. Lang, I, 366–7; copy of the two agreements, dated 20 October 1825, held by the firm of John Murray, Publishers, hereafter cited as Murray Papers; Scott, *Familiar Letters*, II, 356.

10. The 'Noctes Ambrosianae' (loosely, nights at Ambrose's tavern) were published in *Blackwood's* between March 1822 and February 1835. Like the 'Letters of Timothy Tickler' they were written collectively, and consisted of high-spirited, sometimes outrageous criticism and comment. For many they epitomized the spirit of the Magazine.

11. Scott, *Letters*, IX, 249n., 297–300, 304n.1; XII, 454–6.; *Familiar Letters*, II, 369. Smiles, II, 220–4.

12. *Familiar Letters*, II, 359, 416; Scott, *Letters*, IX, 332; Disraeli, *Letters*, I, 51; Smiles, II, 227; Southey, *New Letters*, II, 288.

13. Smiles, II, 220–1; Disraeli, *Letters*, I, 53.

14. Lockhart to Croker, 16 November [1825], quoted by Lott, p.70; Scott, *Letters*, IX, 302.

15. Lockhart to Croker, 19 November 1825, quoted by Lott, p.72; quoted by M. F. Brightfield, *John Wilson Croker* (London: Allen & Unwin, 1940), p.186, hereafter cited as Brightfield.

16. Disraeli, *Letters*, I, 53-55.

17. Quoted by Brightfield, p.188.

18. Scott, *Familiar Letters*, II, 414–6.

19. Smiles, II, 225–9.

20. For a different interpretation of Croker's role in the editorship fracas,

see Charles C. Nickerson, 'Disraeli, Lockhart and Murray: an Episode in the History of the Quarterly Review', *Victorian Studies*, XV (1972), 279–306.

21. Brightfield, p.188; Scott, *Letters*, IX, 290 and 290n.; Lott, p.73; Smiles, II, 217.

22. On the plans for *The Representative* see Robert Blake, *Disraeli* (London: Eyre and Spottiswoode, 1966), pp.29–34, and Scott, *Familiar Letters*, II, 406–10. On the name of the paper see Smiles, II, 206.

23. Nickerson (see note 20) points out that if the dispute between Murray and Disraeli had been only financial Isaac d'Israeli would have been drawn in more than he was as the younger Disraeli was still a minor and not legally responsible for financial matters.

24. Part I was published on 22 April 1826, Part II on 23 February 1827. Blake, pp.37–49, gives a full account of the novel and the circumstances of publication. The Marquess of Carabas was generally agreed to have been based on Murray. Disraeli extensively revised the novel in 1853, omitting many of the offensive passages.

25. The relationship with Monmouth was intended to reflect Croker's dubious connection with the Marquis of Hertford, whose notorious womanizing made him the subject of considerable scandal. Croker was widely believed to have inherited money from Hertford. Rigby, we are told, 'wrote his lampoons and articles; massacred a she liberal ... cut up a rising genius whose politics were different from his own.' See *Coningsby* (London: John Lane, 1905), Bk. 1. Ch. 1, p.15; Blake, p.48.

26. Scott, *Letters*, IX, 333.

27. Scott, *Letters*, IX, 252; See also *The Journal of Sir Walter Scott*, 2 vols (Edinburgh: David Douglas, 1890), I, 24, 309.

28. Scott, *Letters*, IX, 226n and 287n.; *The Private Letter-Books of Sir Walter Scott*, ed. Wilfred Partington (London: Hodder and Stoughton, 1930), p.149.

29. Mrs Gordon, *Christopher North, a Memoir of John Wilson*, 2 vols (Edinburgh: Edmonston and Douglas, 1862), II, 105. Oriel College, Oxford, was to become the base of the nascent Tractarian movement. Newman, Pusey, Hurrell Froude and Keble were fellows in the 1820s, and the *Quarterly* in the 1840s was strongly supportive of the Oxford movement.

30. Scott, *Letters*, IX, 413n and 434n.1. See also Scott, *Private Letter-Books*, pp.147, 355.

31. Lockhart to Murray, 7 February 1826, Murray Papers.

32. Murray urged Scott to use his influence with the old *Quarterly* contributors to quash the opposition to Lockhart so that instead of becoming the 'mere successor to Mr. C.', Lockhart 'would be installed rather in the throne of Gifford'. (draft, Murray Papers).

33. Letter nd. marked 'Mr. Lockhart & editing of *Quarterly*, 1828', Murray Papers.

34. See *The Croker Papers: The Correspondence and Diaries of the late Rt. Hon. John Wilson Croker*, ed. Louis L. Jennings, 3 vols (London: John Murray, 1884), I, 314. In the *Letters*, Scott denounced the proposal to prohibit the circulation of Scottish banknotes below the value of £5. Croker replied under a pseudonym in the *Courier*. In the end the proposal was withdrawn.

35. Lockhart to Murray, 18 May 1828, 19 January, 21 February 1829, Murray Papers; *Despatches, Correspondence and Memoranda of Field Marshall Arthur Duke of Wellington*, 8 vols (London: John Murray, 1867–1880), V, 430–33; Smiles, II, 269–70.

36. Scott, *Letters*, XI, 140. On Catholic Emancipation and the *Quarterly*, see Scott Bennett, 'Catholic Emancipation, the *Quarterly Review* and Britain's Constitutional Revolution', *Victorian Studies*, XII (1969), 283–304.

37. Lockhart–Croker Correspondence, *Notes and Queries*, 25 August 1945; Lockhart to Murray, 15 July 1830, Murray Papers.

38. Lockhart to Murray, 13 September 1831, Murray Papers.

39. See Brightfield, p.404; *The Wellesley Index to Victorian Periodicals*, ed. W. E. Houghton, 4 vols (Toronto: University of Toronto Press, 1966–88), I, 713-16, lists thirty-five articles by Croker between December 1832 and April 1835.

40. See *Croker Papers*, II, 288.

41. Croker to Lockhart, 23 January [1835], quoted by Davis, p.41; Brightfield, p.427.

42. Lockhart to Croker, 9 August [1844], quoted by Lewis, p.230.

43. Croker to Lockhart, 19 November 1825, Lockhart to Croker, 16 July 1837, quoted by Lott, pp.74, 199.

44. Sir John Walsh (1798–1881), author of several pamphlets on parliamentary reform; see DNB; Croker to Murray, 20 February 1836, Murray Papers.

45. Lockhart–Croker Correspondence, *Notes and Queries*, 25 September 1943.

46. Lockhart–Croker Correspondence, *Notes and Queries*, 25 September 1943, 18 November 1944.

47. Despite their differences, Lockhart and Croker were part of a select group of Murray's oldest friends who were asked to attend his funeral by Mrs Murray and her daughters. The others were Sir Francis Head, his doctor, and members of the Stationers Company. BL Add. MSS. 41125 f.75.

48. Lockhart–Croker Correspondence, *Notes and Queries*, 9 October 1943.

49. John Sterling (1806–1844), was an active reviewer, writing for the *Athenaeum*, *Blackwood's*, the *London and Westminster*. While at Cambridge, he had been a member of the Apostles. See DNB. For the context of Croker's and Sterling's reviews, see Edgar F. Shannon, *Tennyson and the Reviewers* (Cambridge, Mass.: Harvard University

Press, 1952, repr. 1967), chs. 1–3.

50. Harriet Martineau, *Biographical Sketches 1852–1868* (London: Macmillan, 1870), pp.376, 378.

51. *Harriet Martineau's Autobiography* with Memorials by M. W. Chapman, 3 vols (London: Smith, Elder, 1877), I, 204–7; Croker to Murray 5 October [1838], Murray Papers.

52. See G. L. Gleig, 'Life of Lockhart', *Quarterly Review*, CXVI, (October 1864) 467–8, and P. H. Stanhope, *Historical Essays contributed to the Quarterly Review*, 2 vols (London, 1849).

53. Croker to Murray, 17 April 1833, Murray Papers.

54. Croker to Lockhart, 27 January [1833], quoted by Davis, p.35.

55. Macaulay, *Letters*, IV, 89–91; Brightfield, p.359.

56. Lockhart to Croker, 24 April 1835, quoted by Lott, p.166; Croker to Lockhart, 10 June 1835, quoted by Davis, p.44; Croker to Murray, 10 April 1832, Lockhart to Murray, 15 May 1835, Murray Papers; Brightfield, p.380.

57. See George Paston, *At John Murray's; Records of a Literary Circle 1843–1892* (London: John Murray, 1932), p.103.

58. Lockhart–Croker Correspondence, *Notes and Queries*, 9 October 1943, 4 November 1844; Lockhart to Croker, 8 July 1840, quoted by Lewis, p.42; Lockhart to Croker, 20 June 1832, quoted by Lott, p.109.

59. Croker to Lockhart, 20 November 1842, quoted by Davis, p.85.

60. Lockhart to Murray, [18?], October 1841, Murray Papers.

61. Lockhart to Croker, 15 November 1843 quoted by Lewis, p.183; Brightfield, p.429.

Chapter 4

MANAGING THE QUARTERLIES

Cockburn's somewhat melancholy reflection on the death of Macvey Napier, that the editorial function of delivering others was apt to impair or at least to supersede one's own creative powers, echoed Lockhart's wearied comment to Murray in 1841 that after fifteen years in the job he had come to realize that an editor almost never received any of the credit for his labours. By the end of their careers, both Napier and Lockhart had become battle-worn and disillusioned as to the dignity and worth of their calling, if indeed it deserved the term. Their view, derived from experience, ran counter to the general image of the editor in the early to mid-nineteenth century, an image, as Bagehot pointed out, which had been transformed by Jeffrey. Jeffrey had 'invented the trade of editorship'. Before him an editor had been 'a bookseller's drudge'. He was now 'a distinguished functionary'.[1]

As with all the early *Edinburgh* reviewers, success and notoriety had created their own legend and Jeffrey's talents and achievement gained recognition retrospectively. But John Gross was right when he commented that at the end of his career, when the achievements were noted and the eulogies written, it was Francis Jeffrey, the editor, rather than Lord Jeffrey, the judge and Lord Advocate, who was best remembered.[2]

Henry Cockburn, not the most impartial of biographers,

nevertheless accurately highlighted Jeffrey's editorial achievement:

> He had to discover and to train, authors; to discern what truth and the
> public mind required; to suggest subjects; to reject, and, more offensive
> still, to improve, contributions; to keep down absurdities; to infuse spirit;
> to excite the timid; to repress violence; to soothe jealousies; to quell
> mutinies; to watch times; and all this in the morning of the reviewing day,
> before experience had taught editors conciliatory firmness, and
> contributors reasonable submission.[3]

Cockburn's point was Bagehot's, that Jeffrey invented the job, that
he had to feel his way, to handle highly idiosyncratic, not to say
egocentric, colleagues, to carve out a policy on various fronts, not
only the political, which would win the consent of all — in other
words to establish a corporate voice from amongst a group of
wayward and sometimes intractable individualists.

The code of anonymity, however thin it became, was the crucial
factor. For John Morley, writing as editor of the *Fortnightly Review*,
in a different reviewing climate when signature had become the norm,
the quarterly editor in the early days was to be envied for the unity of
conviction which had inspired him and his colleagues. It made the
editor's job challenging, sometimes almost impossible, but it also
gave it its main interest:

> With responsibility — not merely for commas and niceties and literary
> kickshaws, but in its old sense — disappears also a portion of the interest
> of editorial labour... It is the cohesion of a political creed that is gone, and
> the strength and fervour of a political school. The principles that inspired
> that group of strong men have been worked out.[4]

The periodicals of the 1860s and 1870s no longer had a binding creed
in quite the same way. The editor's role was to encourage and
promote the 'open pulpit', the 'forum' which had its benefits, but the
old dominant position of the editor had disappeared, Morley
thought.

The magisterial editorial role, as Morley also knew, could be a
constant headache. His analogy was to the manager of an opera
house, the job 'usually supposed to tax human powers more urgently
than any position save that of a general in the very heat and stress of
battle'. The editor of a major periodical was 'the impresario of men of
letters', and was tested in much the same way:

The rival house may bribe his stars. His popular epigrammatist is sometimes as full of humours as a spoiled soprano. The favourite pyrotechnist is systematically late and procrastinatory, or is piqued because his punctuation or his paragraphs have been meddled with. The contributor whose article would be in excellent time if it did not appear before the close of the century, or never appeared at all, pesters you with warnings that a month's delay is a deadly blow to progress and stays the great procession of the ages. The contributor who would profitably fill a sheet, insists on sending a treatise.[5]

It was a scenario which both Napier and Lockhart would have recognized, and would have relished. Jeffrey was the first to admit the precariousness of his position at the supposed head of a factious not to say fractious band of reviewers. He constantly stressed his limited powers. 'I am but a feudal monarch at best, and my throne is overshadowed by the presumptuous crests of my nobles,' he wrote to Horner in 1810; 'I would give a great deal for a few chieftains of a milder and more disciplined character.'

And yet, as Cockburn described it, it was towards Jeffrey that the group gravitated. He became their natural centre. He 'directed and controlled the elements he presided over with a master's judgment. There was not one of his associates who could have even held these elements together for a single year.'[6] Jeffrey's skill in mediating opinions and in establishing, however tenuously, the illusion of unanimity and consistency, was matched, legend had it, by his talents in the less cerebral, nuts-and-bolts aspects of editing. Cockburn described his 'dexterity' in revising the writings of others:

> Without altering the general tone or character of the composition, he had great skill in leaving out defective ideas or words, and in so aiding the original by lively or graceful touches, that reasonable authors were surprised and charmed on seeing how much better they looked than they thought they would.[7]

The word 'reasonable' in this context was likely to have been significant. Jeffrey's skills in this direction were obviously well known at an early stage, for Scott, advising Gifford of an editor's duties, cited Jeffrey's genius in accepting contributions from reviewers who knew their subject but who wrote in 'a tone of stupifying mediocrity', which Jeffrey then 'rendered palatable' by 'throwing in a few lively paragraphs or entertaining illustrations of his own'.[8] One of the most celebrated recipients was still smarting several years later. Writing to Napier in November 1830 Carlyle nursed painful memories of Jeffrey's editorial labours:

> My respected Friend, your Predecessor had some difficulty with me in adjusting the respective prerogatives of Author and Editor: for tho' not as I hope, insensible to fair reason, I used sometimes to rebel against what I reckoned mere authority; and this partly perhaps as a matter of literary conscience, being wont to write nothing without studying it if possible to the bottom, and writing always with an almost painful feeling of scrupulosity, that light Editorial hacking and hewing to right and left was in general nowise to my mind.[9]

In view of Carlyle's subsequent treatment at Napier's hands and the general response to 'Characteristics', he was scarcely better off under the new regime than the old.

Jeffrey's most significant contribution to the role of editor was to make it a gentlemanly pursuit. The amateurism which characterized the first *Edinburgh* reviewers, and the amateurism which Leslie Stephen had deplored, did have the effect of conferring status on journalism. Jeffrey and his colleagues epitomized the concept of gentlemanly amateurism. None of them considered either politics or letters to be his main career. The original intention was that they should be unpaid until Constable persuaded them to accept his fees, fees which were to reflect the professional status of the writer, rather than the standard remuneration of Grub Street. The fees included a substantial honorarium to the editor, £400 in Jeffrey's case. Scott explained the subtlety of the situation to Gifford:

> The Editor to my knowledge acts on the principle that even Czar Peter working in the trenches must accept the pay of a common soldier. This general rule removes all scruple or delicacy & fixes in his service a number of contributors who might otherwise have felt reluctance to accept of compensation for their labours even the more because that compensation was a matter of convenience to them. There are many young men of talent & enterprise who are extremely glad of a handsome apology to work for fifteen or twenty guineas, upon whose gratuitous contributions no reliance could be placed & who nevertheless would not degrade themselves by being paid labourers in a work where others wrote for honour alone.[10]

Jeffrey's editorship established yet another precedent, that of the editor-contributor. While organizing, cajoling, pruning, rewriting and moulding his 'feudal barons' into a semblance of unity, he was also reviewing and at a ferocious pace, seventy-nine articles in twenty-six numbers at one point, or an average of one article a month, a practice that he continued even when his legal career made more pressing claims on his time. His amazing energy and the absence of substantial legal employment during his early years undoubtedly made it easier for him to become a contributing editor.

William Gifford, Jeffrey's opposite number at the *Quarterly*, deliberately chose not to write for the Review but devoted himself instead to the task of rewriting and revising the offerings of his contributors. Southey was loud in his protests at what he termed Gifford's 'mutilations', and other colleagues felt equally strongly that he was wasting his time in futile attempts 'to elucidate a rational meaning from the shapeless lumps of criticism laid before him', as one of them put it.[11]

Napier, like Gifford, chose not to write as well as edit, although he had been a contributor in the past. Editing the *Encyclopædia* together with his academic commitments had no doubt seemed sufficient occupation once the *Edinburgh* was added to them.

Lockhart took precisely the opposite decision, prompted by Murray's and Scott's suggestions that he could substantially increase his £1,200 editorial stipend by taking on some reviewing in addition to his editorial duties. Lockhart's contributions more or less matched Croker's in regularity and number in the 1830s, usually one article per number but often more, with four as an occasional maximum. He was an uninspired and on the whole an unenthusiastic reviewer, lacking Croker's terrier-like nose for a quarrel or a particular angle or even his mischievous sense of sport.

The conjunction within the *Edinburgh* of political conviction backed by political authority on the one hand, and an extremely high degree of articulateness, cleverness and confidence on the other, was essential to its success under Jeffrey and throughout most its history, at least until the 1840s. The sense of purpose and conviction so envied by John Morley was the result of close links between the early reviewers and key figures in the Whig opposition, links carefully nurtured by Jeffrey and used with great sensitivity. Jeffrey's advice to Napier at the height of his struggles with Brougham, on the considerations which should be brought to bear on the admission or rejection of political articles, was cited by Morley as a model of editorial wisdom:

> There are three legitimate considerations by which you should be guided in your conduct as Editor generally, and particularly as to the admission or rejection of important articles of a political sort. 1. The effect of your decision on the other contributors upon whom you mainly rely; 2. its effect on the sale and circulation, and on the just authority of the work with the great body of its readers; and, 3. your own deliberate opinion as to the safety or danger of the doctrines maintained in the article under consideration, and its tendency either to promote or retard the practical adoption of those liberal principles to which, and *their practical advancement*, you must always consider the journal as devoted.[12]

As Jeffrey's successor, Napier was in many ways a disappointment. He lacked the status and the charisma of his predecessor and he lacked his prodigious talents, both intellectual and managerial. His main advantage was that it fell to him to translate the *Edinburgh* from its role as an opposition journal to that of a government organ. His personality and instincts were neither those of a political lobbyist or of a man of affairs. He was an academic of a somewhat stolid kind, and the editor of an encyclopædia, neither of which were posts which brought him in touch with the world of affairs. London to him was a foreign capital. He made annual visits throughout his editorship, usually combining the visits with medical treatment, and he kept in touch through a web of correspondents who transmitted political gossip and substantive information as it came their way.

Macaulay and Empson were vital to the political management of the Review. Napier deferred to the former as to a gifted son whose reflected glories brought their own honour. As time went on their personal relationship deepened. Macaulay was generous and supportive, and an increasingly effective lead into government circles. Empson acted as an unofficial sub-editor, keeping his finger on both the pulse of London literary life and also on political developments. Carlyle's comical picture of Empson as a dishevelled man in a flannel dressing gown, with a wrinkled face, 'large mild melancholy dreamy blue-eyes under bushy brows' and 'in the threshold of mysticism', suggested vagueness and otherworldliness, which was the case, but it cloaked a shrewdness which served Napier well over the years. His contacts were wide, and these as well as Macaulay's, compensated for Napier's deficiencies in this respect.

Harriet Martineau, on the other hand, found Empson a hopeless waverer. He was not capable of having opinions, she thought, and he was, as was usual in such cases, disposed to be afraid of those who had:

> He was in a perpetual course of being swayed about by the companions of the day on all matters but politics. There he was safe; for he was hedged in on every side by the dogmatic Whigs, who made him their chief dogmatist.

It was a nicely barbed observation from one who on the whole had been well treated by the *Edinburgh*. According to her autobiography Empson was wont to bemoan Napier's entire want of literary faculty or cultivation.[13]

Whatever his private doubts and his own deficiencies, Empson proved a stalwart throughout Napier's editorship. It is difficult to imagine how Napier could have proceeded without him. And in the background there was of course Jeffrey, 'quacking himself and amusing us all as usual', as Macaulay recorded. Only moderately successful in his new role of Lord Advocate, Jeffrey occasionally slipped back into the old one, acting as a kind of Emeritus Editor and as the ultimate arbiter in difficult situations.

Brougham of course saw himself in the role of political editor, the success of which has already been demonstrated. 'He is a pretty person truly to advise you & inform you what is useful or agreeable to Ministers in yr. Review,' as Empson commented at the end of one fraught period. But given the support of Empson, Macaulay and Jeffrey and in spite of his trials with Brougham Napier could hardly fail to lead the Review to a position of strength, at least in the first four years of the Whig government. The *Edinburgh*'s profile was high in the mid-1830s. Miss Martineau was less impressed by Napier's political stewardship, claiming that it was widely understood that both he and later Empson inserted all articles sent by Whig ministers or their 'underlings' as a matter of course, however much they might contradict one another even in the same number.[14] It was a good story, and not without a kind of truth, suggesting as it did that the *Edinburgh*, whatever its reputation, no longer had an authoritative figure at its helm, one who was in full control of the Review's political policy.

Scott's ideas about editorship, as he outlined them to Gifford, were unquestionably modelled on Jeffrey. It was Jeffrey's tight control of the Review, his skill in transforming mediocre material into good journalism and above all his political acumen in securing for the *Edinburgh* direct lines of communication with inner opposition circles that he urged Gifford to emulate. The same reasoning was behind his determined efforts, seventeen years later, to smooth Lockhart's entry into political circles. As with Lockhart, he made little headway.

Gifford was singularly ill-equipped to master-mind a party organ. He was thought to have been selected chiefly through Canning's influence, but most of the *Quarterly*'s supporters and Murray himself were quick to point out that although he was a man of learning and wit, he had 'lived too little in the world', as Murray told Scott.[15] His interests were essentially literary, not political, and this factor was crucial to the operation of the *Quarterly*, not only under his editorship, but under his successors. It meant that from the beginning there was a separation of the political from the literary activities of the Review, with Croker more or less in charge of the former. It meant, too, that there was not a single chain of command, and that the Review was almost always run by a combination of people, a triumvirate as with Lockhart, Murray and Croker or, as previously, Croker, Gifford and Murray. In other words, the *Quarterly* editors never had the power and authority enjoyed by their counterparts at the *Edinburgh*.

The supposed unsuitability and otherworldliness of the *Quarterly*'s editors was a source of particular delight in *Edinburgh* circles. MacCulloch met Lockhart for the first time at dinner in 1833 and reported that he looked old, and had 'no quality whatever to fit him for being the editor of a political journal', and that his footing in the *Quarterly* was rumoured to be anything but firm. It was as well that the situation continued, he added with a degree of cynicism. Henry Reeve, a former *Times* leader writer and a man who prided himself that at the age of twenty-six he was personally acquainted with all members of the cabinet except two, coincided in his editorship of the *Edinburgh* from 1855 with Whitwell Elwin at the *Quarterly*. Elwin was a bookish, eccentric and reclusive clergyman, whom Reeve described, with perplexity mixed with slight contempt, as 'a Norfolk parson, of immense reading, great knowledge of books, and great ignorance of the world; evidently unversed in politics and society', in other words just what one had come to expect from the *Quarterly*. The mythology was of course comforting, even if partly invented. By way of balance, Croker's viperishness and power within the *Quarterly* were also distorted out of all semblance to reality, so that there was never a serious belief, in the *Edinburgh* camp, that the *Quarterly* was a toothless tiger, in spite of the bookishness or languid public pose of its editors.[16]

The question of editorial prerogative, of alterations, and more seriously, of 'interpolations' was a perennially vexed one, as successive editors were to discover to their cost. Activist editors made almost instant enemies, as Napier nearly found with Macaulay, although his anxious advisers helped to avert a breach. The limitations of monarchy, to adapt Jeffrey's analogy, were everywhere apparent.

Here too legend undoubtedly embroidered the truth. Scott's, and later Cockburn's, accounts of Jeffrey's transformation of unpromising material have become part of the lore of editing. And so has Gifford's severity as an editor, as Southey's well-publicized protests testified. 'No future Editor, be he who he may, must expect to exercise the same discretion over my papers which Mr. Gifford has done,' he was quoted as saying after the latter's departure.[17] According to Andrew Lang, one of the most worrying symptoms of Gifford's declining health towards the end of his editorship was the publication of one of Southey's articles without corrections, another legendary editorial joke.

Henry Reeve claimed to offer no book for review which he had not read himself, in order to keep tabs on his reviewers — an unlikely story, but it illustrated his assiduity. He too gained a reputation for excessive alteration, to 'sin Reevishly' as the historian E. A. Freeman termed this dubious skill. Whitwell Elwin, like Gifford, was obsessive about detail, claiming to rewrite three out of every four articles in proof. According to his biographer, one irritated contributor returned a cheque, claiming that his article, when it eventually appeared, was not recognizably his at all.[18]

Whatever he may have lacked in forcefulness of personality, Napier had no hesitation in altering his contributors' manuscripts. His experience with the *Encyclopædia Britannica* served him well. His early brush with Macaulay was not something he chose to repeat, but Hazlitt's article on William Ellery Channing, in his first number, was sent back with suggested changes to the introduction. T. J. Hogg complained that the cuts in his article on the Byzantine Historians, also in Napier's first number, 'far exceeded the fair exercise of the privilege of a liberal editor'.[19] Other contributors proved more tractable. Henry Rich, a young politician who was to become a valued reviewer, thanked Napier warmly for his friendly remarks concerning his style and said he would endeavour to profit from them. Empson thought Napier had made the corrections in one of his articles better than he could have done himself. Macaulay's friend Thomas Flower Ellis professed himself unflustered by Napier's alterations and confessed he would have liked *more* excisions. Only Carlyle refused to cut half a page from the text of 'Corn-Law Rhymes', claiming that no passage could be cut 'without great loss of blood',[20] and suggesting that if Napier were desperate, some of the extracts from Elliott's poems could be omitted. The article was published without cuts. This apart, the general tenor of Napier's correspondence suggested no resentment or confrontation over what appeared on the whole to be reasonable changes.

The problem of lengthy articles was a general anxiety to all quarterly editors. The opposition to Napier's initiative to reduce the length of articles underlined a widespread belief that the quarterlies existed to give reviewers scope for expansiveness denied to them by other periodical forms. The advent of magazines like *Blackwood's*, and *Fraser's* in their more sober moments, and others like *Tait's Edinburgh Magazine* as well as weeklies like the *Athenaeum* and the *Spectator*, was a salutary reminder that it was possible to write serious reviews within a smaller compass. Napier was right in spotting the dangers of what was in effect the absence of restrictions on length. Reviews of forty or even fifty pages were regularly submitted and editors did little more than wring their hands. Croker too had spotted the dangers and groaned to Murray in 1823 that 'this cursed system of writing dissertations will be the death of us'.[21] He vowed that if he were ever in charge of a Review he would scarcely permit an article to exceed a single sheet of sixteen pages, an interesting comment from one who was to submit an eighty-page review of Macaulay's *History*.

Most reviewers would have none of the argument for curtailment. MacCulloch warned Napier that if he persisted with his policy he would ruin the Review in the process, and that people who wanted only to 'skim the surface' of a subject would go instead to the magazines. Bowring had tried the same thing with the *Westminster* and instead of increasing sales had sunk the journal to the level of a magazine and destroyed it. Macaulay thought it essential when tackling a subject which tended to branch out in many directions that a reviewer should not feel constrained by length, and suggested a mixture of ten or twelve short articles and two or three long ones.[22]

Neither Napier nor Lockhart had much success in reducing the length of articles. In 1834 Croker again urged Lockhart to confine his contributors to two sheets and to increase the total number of articles to fourteen or fifteen, but the suggestion made little impact. When Macaulay's essay on Bacon (July 1837) ran to over one hundred pages and Napier murmured about cuts, it was Jeffrey who protested: 'What mortal could even dream of cutting out the least particle of this precious work to make it fit better into your Review? It would be worse than paring down the Pitt diamond to fit the old setting of a dowager's ring.'[23] The prospect of returning to the early days of between twenty and thirty short reviews faded almost as quickly as it had been raised. It was a mistake which was to have serious repercussions for the future of the quarterlies.

The popular and widespread belief that Lockhart and Croker regularly and liberally interpolated their own views and comments into the pages of the *Quarterly*, unknown to the contributors, has been shown to have been for the most part exaggerated. Harriet Martineau's story of Croker's dinner party threats and of Lockhart's late night sally to the printers to remove offensive material (see above p. 65) was the product of an overheated imagination brooding over old grievances. That said, the so-called 'Mahonscrape', in Croker's word, did occur. And it is likely too that Croker inserted some prefatory material into Poulett Scrope's April 1833 article on Miss Martineau and possibly into Coulton's June 1852 article. Croker may well have tinkered with other articles. Small insertions and changes either by Lockhart or by Croker appear to have been standard *Quarterly* practice, and it was regarded by both as a normal procedure.

Croker himself was unrepentant and unembarrassed about the Mahon affair (see pp. 65-6). He regarded it as an awkward incident, which might compromise the very existence of the Review. Writers contributed to reviews with certain things understood, he told Murray, alterations or even interpolations being one of them. He instanced one of his own articles, on parliamentary and church reform in December 1832, which had been tacked on to another article by a different author (Henry Phillpotts): 'Had I any right to complain & appeal to the public against Mr. Lockhart's decisions?' When he enlisted a new 'hand' the other day, he had told him forthrightly that he must expect to see alterations and even mutilations but that such were 'the condition of our bond'.[24]

For Croker and for Lockhart, it was not a case of the exposure of dirty tricks, but a matter of the rules of the game. The game, as they saw it, was rougher than the one envisaged by a newer generation of reviewers who had not cut their teeth in the *Blackwood* era or in the early days of the *Edinburgh* and the *Quarterly*, when the secrets of the printing house *were* secrets. Here, of course, the erosion of the principle of anonymity had had an effect. It is unlikely that an injured party in Lord Mahon's circumstances would have so obviously publicized his wounds twenty or even ten years previously. The 'Mahonscrape' in 1833 nicely demonstrated the changing climate — from one in which editorial power was absolute and all secrets were kept, when, as Morley would have it, editor and contributors were bound together by conviction, to a new era in which anonymity was a pretence, gamely upheld, but a practice in which no one seriously believed any longer.

Jeffrey's plea to John Allen in 1825 for some 'clever young man', who could write for the *Edinburgh*, coupled with his additional reflection that the original supporters were getting old and were either too busy, too Tory or too stupid, illustrated a perennial editorial predicament. The process of finding likely new reviewers was more difficult than it might at first have seemed. For John Morley, the advent of signed articles meant the removal of one treasured editorial freedom, that of recruiting an unknown young reviewer, a Macaulay recently down from Cambridge, or the young and obscure Carlyle. The editor of a signed publication was forced to go for established names. His predecessors in the 1830s would have acknowledged the advantage of being able to recruit unknown but promising writers, but would have emphasized the scarcity of talent. A young Macaulay or Carlyle did not emerge on an annual basis. For that matter, Morley himself believed that even in his day, with such a demand for periodical writers, there was 'no risk of a literary candle remaining long under a bushel'.[25]

Most new reviewers came on the personal recommendation of established reviewers and supporters. Macaulay, Empson, Jeffrey and MacCulloch, to name the most active *Edinburgh* recruiters, put names forward and Napier in most cases acted upon their suggestions. Exceptionally, Thomas Lister, a young novelist and political aspirant, wrote to Napier in April 1830 with the offer of an article on Delavigne's *Marino Faliero* fearing, he said, that he might be guilty of presumption. He was lucky. The proffered article filled a niche and cemented for Lister a steady connection with the Review. The majority of articles submitted in this way, and without a powerful patron, did not appear.

The normal agreements between the would be contributor and the editor were in principle only, with contributors suggesting areas in which they would like to review, and sometimes mentioning areas they could or would not undertake. Having established an unofficial territory, they then approached the editor with suggestions of books or specific subjects in which they were interested.

The process almost never worked in reverse. Most reviewers positively disliked being asked to review a specific book. When Napier suggested that the historian Henry Hallam might review an historial work together with a recent biography, Hallam immediately responded that he did not think habitual reviewing would suit him, especially when the book was suggested by someone else. Similarly, Dionysius Lardner claimed he could not bring himself to write reviews 'to order'. At least, he admitted, this must be his excuse for making offers to Napier instead of waiting to be asked. Brougham was furious in 1835 when in an attempt to attract him to a non-controversial subject, Napier suggested he might like to review a particular book. A petulant Brougham professed outrage that he should have been treated like a 'hack' and ' "offered" such and such books — that is, whatever nobody else wishes to do'. It was particularly wounding to one who had served the Review faithfully for so many years. Southey had not been so shabbily treated by the *Quarterly*, he added. The incident occurred at the peak of Brougham's frenzy over his treatment by Melbourne and an exasperated Napier had merely been trying to occupy him. It was a nice reminder, though, of a principal premise of reviewing, that reviewers 'offered' a subject or a book, while 'hacks' were assigned to a book or a subject.[26]

It made the advanced planning of numbers extremely complicated. Editors canvassed suitable reviewers for controversial, sensitive and important books well in advance of publication. Croker's *Boswell*, the Duke of Wellington's *Despatches*, the *Life of Wilberforce*, the *Life of Sir James Mackintosh*, and Mackintosh's *History of the Revolution*, Lockhart's *Life of Scott*, Macaulay's *Lays of Ancient Rome*, and his *Essays* and the *History* were earmarked by both editors for special attention. There was never a problem over political articles. With contributors like Brougham and Croker plus other interested parties it was more likely to be the case of too many rather than too few reviews.

But the mixture of subjects in any number, the combination of literature, history, biography, religion, travel, art, as well as politics, science, and social and economic questions, depended as much on the reviewers currently available as on editorial decisions on what had been published during a given period, or on what would make a stimulating article. The recruitment of able reviewers and the unending search for thought-provoking, interesting and readable articles was a constant editorial burden.

The jibe that a Review was sinking to the level of a magazine always produced alarm. T. F. Ellis, writing to Napier in November 1837 possibly with the *Quarterly* for October in mind, commented, 'I am heartily glad that you are resolved to preserve the Review from the species of degradation into which others have fallen. I expect every day to read in the *Quarterly* a lively essay with personal sketches upon cock fighting and boxing'.[27] It was not a comment which Lockhart or Murray would have enjoyed. The October 1837 *Quarterly* contained two 'serious' articles, one on the universities, and the other a savage attack by Croker on Lord John Russell, based on one of his recent speeches. The remainder of the issue was made up of three reviews of travel literature, an article on 'Codes of Manners and Etiquette' by Abraham Hayward, and a review of *Pickwick Papers*, also by Hayward. By quarterly standards, this was frivolity indeed. Ellis might easily have made a similar comment on either the *Edinburgh* for July 1838 or the following number for October, both of which contained a large number of 'light' articles, including one on Lady Blessington's novels in July and another on Dickens, by Lister, in October, as well as reviews of current biographies and travel literature.

It was a recognized blindspot in some quarterly editors of this period that reviews of fiction were regarded as light weight and only to be inserted as a last resort. In fact, 'literature' proper, current fiction, poetry and essays, proved more difficult to review than might have been expected. The paucity of both the *Edinburgh* and the *Quarterly*'s reviewing of fiction in the 1840s in comparison with their less illustrious competitors has been noted,[28] and that trend began in the 1830s. Bulwer, who would have been an obvious choice to review novels, pointedly refused to review his friends and colleagues for fear of giving offence or seeming arrogant or, conversely, of being inundated with requests for favourable notices. Macaulay too was reluctant to review literature, considering himself a generalist in reviewing terms, but definitely not a literary critic. He had never written a page of criticism on poetry or the fine arts which he would not burn if he had the power, he told Napier. Croker also fought shy of fiction and poetry when he had an alternative.[29]

Science was also a difficult area. As Lardner pointed out to Napier, few scientists could write well, and even fewer literary men knew enough about science to write without 'falling into gross and ludicrous blunders'. Sir David Brewster advised Napier that there was no point in having scientific reviews unless the reviewer could make them interesting to scientists. Lockhart, on the other hand, claimed that eminent scientists were too egotistical to make good reviewers. 'The devil is that they all think more of shewing themselves off than of conveying knowledge,' he moaned to Croker.[30] All of this suggests that the assumption that science in the nineteenth century was more accessible as a part of general culture and less the preserve of specialists than it is today might be wide of the mark.

Reviewers did have a sense of belonging to a specific Review, however unofficial or indeed nonexistent their contracts. When writing to ask Napier to arrange for a review of his 'little book' , a *Life of Earl Howe*, in 1838, John Barrow felt obliged to mention that he had had no recent contact with either Lockhart or Murray for some time. Basil Hall, the reviewer he requested, and a regular contributor to the *Quarterly*, later got himself into hot water with Napier when he suggested that he might write an article on a book by a friend, a work he had already reviewed in the *Quarterly*. Napier reacted sharply and soon put him right as to the etiquette of reviewing, or rather 'the propriety of different Journals being supplied with independent articles by different hands'. The geographer W. D. Cooley was probably more punctilious than most when he insisted on consulting J. G. Cochrane, then editor of the *Foreign Quarterly* before responding to an approach from Napier to write for the *Edinburgh*. Cochrane made no objection, but reserved the right of veto, which he presumably did not exercise, as Cooley became a regular contributor to the *Edinburgh*. The sense of being a member of a team was undoubtedly encouraged by the political affiliations of the Reviews. As these weakened, reviewers felt less inclined to commit themselves to a single Review and tended to offer their articles to a number of editors, although the *Edinburgh* was usually the first port of call.[31]

Editors were sometimes approached directly by authors eager for notice in a particular review. Lobbying of varying degrees of subtlety was expected, even in this post puffing era. G. P. R. James, the historical novelist, sent Napier a copy of his *History of Charlemagne*, published by Longman. He had not given the book to Henry Colburn, a publisher notorious for puffing his authors, he told Napier, as he had not wanted to see it 'puffed like Warren's Blacking',[32] and he had no doubt that in Longman's hands it would obtain the place in literature it deserved. This may indeed have happened, but even the Longman connection could not secure it a notice in the *Edinburgh*. Thomas Lister, however, probably benefited from being a reviewer when he modestly pressed the case of his novel *Arlington*, which was reviewed in the October 1832 issue. He also requested that Empson review his *Life of Clarendon*, sensing that the review would be sympathetic. As the work had been savaged by Croker in the *Quarterly* Napier readily granted the request. John Allen was embarrassed to have to forward a work on Greco-Egyptian antiquities which the Dutch Ambassador had sent to him with the request that he do his best to have it noticed in the *Edinburgh*. Despite his good connections, the ambassador's protégé was not given the benefit of notice in the Review.

On the face of it, the planning of each number of the *Edinburgh* seemed to have been haphazard in the extreme. Napier had on his books a sizeable number of names: Brougham, Macaulay, Empson, Lister, Henry Rich, MacCulloch, the philosopher William Hamilton, the scientist Sir David Brewster, and later Herman Merivale, on whom he could call regularly for articles. In addition he had others, T. J. Hogg, Carlyle, Dionysius Lardner, Thomas Spring-Rice, Henry Cockburn, Thomas Moore, Jeffrey, John Allen, Bulwer Lytton, Thomas Arnold, James Spedding, James Stephen and Francis Palgrave, who all contributed less frequently, but who for certain periods regarded themselves as *Edinburgh* reviewers.

There was never a list of books or subjects drawn up for review or consideration in each number, nor was there a sense of distinct departments with reviewers attached to each. Regular reviewers had a well-developed intuitive sense that certain subjects or books would be most likely to fall to them and proceeded accordingly, so that Napier rarely had to go in search of reviewers. This of course made it difficult for a newcomer to break into the charmed circle, hence one of Carlyle's difficulties in finding appropriate subjects for the *Edinburgh* and one of the reasons for the clash between Brougham and Macaulay in 1830. There was a rough spread of subjects in each issue, at least one political article; sometimes one on economic or legal matters; others on history, science, and art, as well as a variable mixture of lighter subjects, fiction, poetry, biography and travel. An increase in the proportion of 'light' articles was an indication that an editor was in difficulty, and having trouble in securing topical or stimulating material.

There was 'a monstrous charlatanry' about the old editorial 'we', Morley had been drawn to reflect from a later vantage point, and a view into the management of a quarterly, however incomplete, seems only to confirm this assertion. The sense of a unified voice, or of a common cause, as envisaged in the early days of both the *Edinburgh* and the *Quarterly*, is difficult to sense in this erratic, unstructured, hand-to-mouth existence at three-monthly intervals. The increasing thinness of the veil of anonymity, too, made a unified voice less and less of a reality.

What did create cohesion and consistency was the political element, the one or two articles in each number which were directed by immediate events or orchestrated by political sources, and which sparked off the old rivalries of the two Reviews. The old fervour, the conviction and the pugnacious spirit could be fanned into flame in an instant and the ramifications of the debate and the quarrels spread easily to other aspects of the Reviews. Without politics, however, a vital element in the chemistry of quarterly reviewing was missing.

The editorial 'we' had become an element of style so fundamental that most reviewers used it automatically. 'We approach this very remarkable and learned work with extreme diffidence.' 'Although we rarely and unwittingly devote our pages to the discussion of party matters, and what are usually termed the politics of the day, there are times when this becomes a duty.' 'We did not expect a good book from Mr. Sadler; and it is well that we did not; for he has given us a very bad one.' 'We are glad to meet with a respectable specimen of that class of works called "Novels of Fashionable Life", which furnish an extensive and popular part of the light reading of the present day.' 'We shall not on the present occasion enter at large into the recent proceedings of the Society.'

These sentences, each from the opening paragraphs of articles in a single number of the *Edinburgh* (July 1830) affect to speak with a corporate voice, and assume a team spirit and a unity of purpose which is belied by the behind the scenes activity of the Review. The reviewers, T. J. Hogg, Brougham, Macaulay, T. H. Lister. and J. R. MacCulloch, individually paid more than lip service to their role in the Review, and each retained a modicum of affection for it. But they were also capable of obstinacy, egocentricity, outright rebellion, and in Brougham's case, treachery. The force behind the 'we' was often little more than notional.

But charlatanry it was not, or at least only rarely. Brougham's flagrant misuse of the editorial 'we' in his dispute with James Stephen over the latter's review of the *Life of Wilberforce* and Napier's supine connivance, was a striking instance of abuse, as James Stephen was quick to realize (see pp. 32-4). 'We are anxious to correct two inaccuracies into which we find we have fallen in our article', the introductory paragraph of Brougham's end note began (Vol. LXVIII, 188): 'Our statement [regarding the placing of Clarkson's name on the controversial map] was erroneous and we can now only say that we are sorry for the mistake.' The effect, as Brougham intended, was that the apology came from the editor on behalf of the penitent reviewer, when in fact it was the personal view of a separate contributor.

Brougham enjoyed the use of end notes, and this was by no means his first. The celebrated speech on colonial slavery in the summer of 1830, which he had assumed Macaulay would notice in the Review, was previewed by a two-page summary of the speech written by himself in the July issue. Most of the notes of this sort, supposedly written by the editor, related to Brougham's articles, either previews or afterthoughts, which in part explains Napier's wearied acquiescence in the Wilberforce episode. The latter occasion was one of the few instances in which the deception damaged another reviewer.

Consistency was an ever-present concern. Here too Morley thought it 'unfathomable folly' in a periodical to affect eternal consistency and to be careful 'not to talk sense on a given question today because its founders talked nonsense upon it fifty years ago'.[33] Brougham had used precisely the reverse of this argument in connection with Stephen's treatment of Clarkson, that the *Edinburgh* from its foundation had taken a pro-Clarkson line (see above p. 42 n. 24).

Thirty-odd years later, as Morley would have argued, it did not seem to matter very much. What concerned both editors and contributors much more was the readers' short-term memory.

On this point, T. J. Hogg was understandably angry when, after he had reviewed the first volume of Niebuhr's *History of Rome* rather severely in July 1830, another reviewer, Henry Malden, Professor of Greek at London University, was recruited through Macaulay to undertake the second volume in January 1833. Malden somewhat diffidently noted that his view of Niebuhr was 'very different' from that of the author of the first review, which was presumably Napier's intention. Hogg, on the other hand, requested a statement in the next issue to the effect that the two articles were by different contributors. He had never supposed, he told Napier, that anything 'so unusual, unworthy & absurd' could have been intended, as to set one person to criticize one portion of a work and another the remainder. The requested explanation was not printed. Readers probably guessed, from the difference in style and attitude, and from the absence of any reference to the preceding article, that the second review was by a different hand. Henry Crabb Robinson certainly heard the story and noted it in his diary.[34]

Most writers, and one assumes, most readers, were more relaxed about internal consistency. Walter Coulson, who reviewed MacCulloch's *Principles of Political Economy* in January 1831, and was worried that his views might contradict those of his subject, no doubt expressed the sentiments of many when he added that 'the notion of the public that they have a right to consistency in any journal to which many persons of various shades of opinion must contribute has always struck me as a little unreasonable'.[35]

As the force of anonymity receded, with it went some editorial responsibility, but not all. In a situation without signature, someone had to assume authority and there was no doubt that it was the editor. The publication in the *Caledonian Mercury* of a letter from Lord Durham to the Publishers of the *Edinburgh Review* in protest against Brougham's October 1834 article on 'The Last Session of Parliament' (see above p. 31) brought Napier out in all his dignity. Had His Lordship addressed the letter to the Editor rather than to the Publisher:

> I should at once have informed Lord Durham that I was responsible for the article in question; but I should have refused, on any supposition, to tell his Lordship whether I wrote that article myself or not; because had I

done so in his case, I could not refuse to do the like in every other where the question might be put, and would thereby have sacrificed the character and usefulness of the publication committed to my charge.[36]

The sense remained, then, at least in the mid 1830s, that the editor depended on a corporate voice and through it upheld his editorial responsibility.

Gentility appeared to be the order of the day in quarterly circles as far as money was concerned. Murmurs of surprise and gratitude for the 'handsome', 'liberal' or 'generous' terms were regularly conveyed both to Napier and to Murray, suggesting that there was rarely, if ever, dissatisfaction over payment. This was not to suggest that the fee was not an important consideration for reviewers. 'The *Quarterly* has occasional assistance from the rich, but the greater part of its pages comes almost always from persons to whom a £50 note or even a £20 one is of real consequence', Lockhart reminded Croker in 1843.[37]

The general resolve was to pay handsomely in order to reinforce the point that quarterly reviewing was the occupation of gentlemen, not hacks, but also to make it clear that the said gentlemen could make a living by their writing, if they so chose. Southey was a classic case of a writer whose income from reviewing was his mainstay apart from a small pension of £140 which he was given at the age of 55, and a £90 stipend from the Laureateship. He was regularly paid £100 for each article in the *Quarterly* irrespective of length and contracted to write four articles a year, an indication of Murray's esteem and a reward for loyalty and long service.[38]

Murray paid Scott at the same rate of £100 per article for his contributions during the early years of Lockhart's editorship, which contrasted well with the small sums proffered by the newly established *Foreign Quarterly Review*, whose hapless editor, R. P. Gillies, constantly solicited Scott's aid, and for whom he occasionally wrote gratuitously, conscious that he was making a financial sacrifice.[39] Croker found Murray's generosity embarrassing, and on one occasion returned a cheque because he thought the sum too large and because he also knew the Review to be in some financial difficulty.

The finances of the *Quarterly* were entirely Murray's concern.

'You know I have no control as to the Q.R.'s money matters. Murray shews me what he means to do & asks my opinion & I give it but it is seldom that I differ from his programme — never as too narrow,' Lockhart told Croker many years later.[40] Murray's impulsive generosity threw the *Quarterly*'s finances into periodic crises in the 1830s, during which he plunged both himself and Lockhart into despair, but the gloom quickly evaporated. The ledgers from September 1843 to July 1846, the only ones to register income from sales, indicate a profit on average of £500 per issue. The standard rate of payment for the *Quarterly*, according to George Paston, began at £10 per sheet and moved to £12 and then to £16. This is probably an underestimate for the thirties. Murray's payments to stars like Scott, Southey and Croker were more in the range of £40 to £50 per sheet.

The sums entered under the contributors' column in Murray's ledgers for the year 1829 and part of 1830, were sometimes over £800, suggesting more than one article by Southey and sometimes one by Scott. The total figure then dropped sharply to just over £400 in 1831 and averaged £400 for the remainder of the decade. With each issue containing approximately eighteen sheets (288 pages) the average payment was £22 per sheet. The sliding scale was in operation for Southey and Croker, but it was a generous scale of payment none the less and one that must have been the envy of other quarterlies. Crabb Robinson confirmed this as a general impression in 1837 when he quoted John Robertson of the *Westminster and London Review* [sic] who assured him that the *Edinburgh* did not now pay its expenses nor regularly paid its contributors, and that the *Quarterly* was the only Review which did.[41].

The agreement signed between Lockhart and Murray in October 1825 specified an editor's fee of £1,200 per annum, £300 per quarter or issue. It was Murray's assumption that Lockhart could increase this figure by £200 to £300 by his own contributions, which most certainly was the case. Lockhart's correspondence, like Croker's and Scott's, recorded his embarrassed gratitude at Murray's constant generosity. The editorial stipend was later raised to £325.

Unlike Murray, Longman kept very much in the background, and allowed Napier to conduct the financial transactions with reviewers. Napier also operated a sliding scale. No payment would be an adequate reward for Macaulay's services, as he was quick to tell him, but he did go beyond the rates of his predecessor. He was paid the equivalent of £30 per sheet for the second and third articles on the Utilitarian controversy in 1829. MacCulloch was paid over £35 for his April 1832 article on precious metals, which was a single sheet in length. Napier reckoned to pay Macaulay, MacCulloch, Empson and one or two other valued regulars at a higher than average rate. Henry Cockburn professed himself embarrassed at Napier's generosity and wished he could be allowed to return his fee in the spring of 1830. Brougham, on the other hand, was business-like, keeping a careful eye on what he was owed until it reached three figures, at which point he gave instructions for the dispatch of a cheque. Hazlitt, who like Southey lived very much from hand to mouth by his journalism, was not embarrassed to ask Napier for an advance. MacCulloch confirmed the disparity between the established quarterlies and their newer competitors, delightedly reporting that the *Foreign Quarterly* paid at the rock-bottom rate of £12 per sheet.

The general sense, from Napier's and other correspondence, is that the *Edinburgh* was less awash with money than the *Quarterly*, which might bear out Crabb Robinson's report, although it still paid at a much higher rate than the newer quarterlies. Longman's proprietorship can scarcely have meant a precarious existence such as the *Westminster* constantly faced under a succession of small proprietors. There is no reference anywhere to Napier's stipend. Scott quoted Moore's Diary for 1823 which claimed that Jeffrey had £700 per annum as editor of the *Edinburgh*, which was substantially less than Murray's offer to Lockhart two years later. Gillies was said to receive £500 for editing the *Foreign Quarterly*, a large sum considering the Review's generally precarious finances.[42]

Circulation figures are patchy for both quarterlies. Writing to Peel in May 1828 Scott informed him that the *Quarterly* sold 12,000 annually, and that 2,000 of these had been added under the present editorship. He claimed that the *Quarterly*'s circulation was more than all the other Reviews, including the *Edinburgh*, and confirmed the figure to Sir William Knighton, the King's private secretary, in September, adding that the *Edinburgh* did not sell 6,000 nor did all the rest of the quarterlies put together.[43]

Murray's ledgers, which begin in January 1829, show a print run of 10,750, significantly below Scott's figure less than six months later. The 10,750 figure dropped to 10,500 for April 1829 where it remained until November 1831, when it dropped further to 9,000, possibly because there were five issues published in that year. It returned briefly to 10,000 for part of 1832 and then wavered around 9,000, 9,250 and 9,500 for the rest of the decade, never returning to the 10,000 mark. Sales figures, as opposed to a print run, are given in the ledgers for the period 1840 to July 1846 and show a figure which remained fairly steady at just over 9,000, until the end of 1844, when sales of below 9,000 are intermittently recorded, going as low as 8,549 in July 1846, the last date in the ledger. In addition, it was customary to reprint certain issues which contained successful or controversial articles, often political ones. Murray reprinted between 250 and 300 copies in most cases, which added to the total circulation figure. Sometimes only the article itself was reprinted for wider circulation.

From the early 1840s onwards, when the excesses of international piracy had been curbed, it was customary to print an additional 100 to 250 copies for distribution in America. Often these were sent in sheets to be bound by the American distributor, which in Murray's case was Wiley and Putnam. Prior to this arrangement, all American 'editions' of the *Edinburgh*, the *Quarterly*, and most other periodicals were in fact pirated versions, distinguished by their double columns of print.[44] In addition to the American copies, Murray's ledgers record a further 150 to 200 'colonial' copies, for despatch to British colonies.

In spite of American and colonial editions and special printings, the general trend was clear — a gradual decrease in the print run from the end of 1832, when it fell below 10,000, and a corresponding decrease in the mid-1840s when the sales figures dropped below 9,000. The figures were still high in comparison with the reported circulation of newer quarterlies like the *North British*, established in 1844, and the *British Quarterly*, founded the following year, which considered themselves viable with a circulation of just over 2,000. According to Brougham, the *British and Foreign Review*, established in 1835, sold 1,000 in its first weeks, which was regarded as good news.[45]

There are no comparable figures for the *Edinburgh*, unfortunately, as Longman's ledgers are no longer in existence, but it is likely that in terms of print run it lagged slightly behind the *Quarterly*, as it had done traditionally for some time. Longman told Napier in 1837 that although the situation was not as good as it had been, the circulation figures were holding their own and he was reasonably satisfied.

In the prologue to the first volume of *The Rise and Fall of the Political Press in Britain* Stephen Koss quoted Abraham Hayward, an active quarterly reviewer, who advised a Peelite politician in 1853 that it was 'an error to measure utility by circulation'.[46] Hayward was speaking of the newspaper press and stressing the accessibility of newspapers in clubs and reading rooms, the reprinting of articles from the London press in provincial papers, and the less tangible dissemination of articles and leaders which formed the basis of political speeches and which also furnished topics for general discussion. Koss's point, which was also Hayward's, is that there was no direct correlation between a newspaper's circulation figures and its political influence, and the same could be said of the quarterlies. Print runs give a general indication of circulation, but it is much more difficult to ascertain readership even when sales figures are available. At six shillings, the quarterlies were expensive. They were probably as much read in clubs, libraries and reading rooms as they were at home. And like the newspapers, they formed the basis of widespread discussion. In addition, the standard process of digesting quarterly articles into politically compatible newspapers was another way in which the influence, at least of particular articles, was far more widespread than circulation or sales figures indicated.

The circulation of the two major quarterlies was undoubtedly on the decline in the 1830s. The peak was probably reached in the second decade of the century, when figures of 14,000 were recorded for the *Quarterly* and 13,500 for the *Edinburgh*, before the influx of the magazines and rival quarterlies.[47] The general indications were that the readership of the original two remained strong, if slightly diminished, and that their influence was sustained. But the 1830s was probably the last decade in which this could confidently be claimed.

Four issues per year was the norm for the quarterlies, and the timing of these was important. Gifford had been notoriously late in his delivery of copy, so much so that Murray and also Lockhart were constantly jumpy over deadlines. Great significance was placed on non-appearance, as in the case of Napier's first number, due out in October 1829. When it had still not appeared in mid-December, Macaulay reported anxiously from London that all kinds of rumours were in circulation, which did the Review no good.[48] A delay of one or two days in order to accommodate a vital political piece was justifiable but anything more was a worry.

The *Edinburgh* was published regularly in January, April, July and October. The *Quarterly*'s pattern was more erratic, mainly because Lockhart was faced with a constant backlog of contributions which he dealt with by instigating extra numbers, a policy which neither Murray nor Croker liked. It was frequently the case in the 1830s that the *Quarterly* appeared five times annually. It made a regular cycle impossible, but Lockhart did take pains whenever he could to bring the *Quarterly* out in a different month to the *Edinburgh*, arguing that as most people read both it was important not to have to divide the limelight.

Their political role kept the quarterlies in a central position in the thirties, but once that influence began to ebb, the question of a role and the quality of general reviewing became extremely important. However much they affected to dismiss them, the magazines and other quarterlies proved to be strong competitors, competition which no editor could afford to ignore.

Andrew Lang gave an unglamorous account of Lockhart's editorial chores:

> Endless reading of contributions in manuscript, of books in manuscript, interminable consultations over articles, corrections of articles, interpolation of articles, correspondence with writers of articles, the reading of new books, and the accomplishing of new articles on the new books — often trash, — these things were the daily life of Lockhart, as of able editors in general. A man in his position is engaged in a kind of intellectual egg-dance among a score of sensitive interests. The authors reviewed not to their liking, the authors not reviewed at all, the rejected contributors, the sensitive small-fry of letters, were ready to say and believe anything evil of Lockhart.[49]

James Moncrieff, reviewing Jeffrey's collected *Edinburgh* essays in 1844 made a similar observation:

> For a dull, ill-tempered man, fancy could not imagine a more refined and perfect torment than the life of an editor. Tied to a stake — a mark for every disappointed friend or foe to fling at — daily devoured by the petulance of authors — the jealousies and intolerable delays of contributors, and the grumblings of publishers — and doomed to a task never ending — still beginning — more hopeless and interminable than the labours of the fabled sisters, 'speeding to-day, to be put back tomorrow' — an editor might well require leisure the most uninterrupted, and patience almost patriarchal, if he hoped to enjoy his life, or to retain it long.[50]

Presented in this light, the job of editor was an unattractive prospect. The sheer drudgery, compounded by the need for the resources of an opera house manager, as Morley rightly saw, plus the political contacts and skills of a minor cabinet minister, made it a tall order which few were able to fill. Jeffrey may have invented the trade of editorship. He could also be said to have set a standard and created a model which only someone with his unique combination of talents could successfully achieve.

Notes

1. Walter Bagehot, 'The First Edinburgh Reviewers', *Literary Studies*, 2 vols (London: Longmans, Green, 1884), I, 30.
2. John Gross, *The Rise and Fall of the Man of Letters* (London: Weidenfeld and Nicolson, 1969), p.3.
3. Henry Cockburn, *Life of Lord Jeffrey*, 2 vols (Edinburgh: Adam and Charles Black, 1852), I, 301–2.
4. John Morley, 'Memorials of a Man of Letters', in *Nineteenth-Century Essays*, ed. P. Stansky (London: University of Chicago Press, 1970), p.269.
5. Morley, pp.261–2.
6. *Life of Jeffrey*, I, 295–6; 302.
7. *Life of Jeffrey*, I, 302–3.
8. Scott, *Letters*, II, 104.
9. Carlyle, *Letters*, V, 195.
10. Scott, *Letters*, II, 103.
11. Smiles, I, 163.
12. *Napier*, p.219; quoted by Morley, p.271.
13. Carlyle, *Letters*, V, 379; *Harriet Martineau's Autobiography*, with memorials by Maria Weston Chapman, 3 vols (London: Smith, Elder, 1877), I, 213.
14. Macaulay, *Letters*, I, 273; BL Add. MSS 34618, f.434; Carlyle, *Letters*, V, 310–11; Martineau, *Autobiography*, I, 213.
15. Smiles, I, 109.
16. BL Add. MSS. 34616 f.60; J.K. Laughton, *Memoirs of the Life and Correspondence of Henry Reeve*, 2 vols (London: Longman, 1898), I, 357.
17. Southey, *New Letters*, II, 272.
18. *Letters to a Victorian Editor, Henry Allon*, ed. Albert Peel (London, 1929), p.82.
19. BL Add. MSS 34614, f.259.
20. BL Add. MSS 34615. f.350; Carlyle, *Letters*, VI, 176.

21. Smiles, II, 57.
22. Macaulay, *Letters*, I, 258; BL Add. MSS 34614, f.178.
23. *Napier*, p.191.
24. Croker to Murray, 17 April 1833, Murray Papers.
25. Morley, p.272.
26. BL Add. MSS 34616, f.264; 34617, f.118.
27. BL Add. MSS. 34616, f.378.
28. See Kathleen Tillotson, *Novels of the Eighteen-Forties* (Oxford: Clarendon Press, 1959), p.16 and Richard Stang, *The Theory of the Novel in England 1850–1870* (London: Routledge and Kegan Paul, 1961), pp.46–7.
29. BL Add. MSS 34617, f.155; 34618, f.60; Macaulay, *Letters*, III, 245.
30. BL Add. MSS 34614, f.482; Lockhart to Croker, 27 January 1842, quoted by Lewis, p.102; BL Add. MSS 34616, f.27.
31. BL Add. MSS 34616, f.27; 34619, f.32; 34619, ff.318, 391. See Joanne Shattock, 'Spreading it Thinly: Some Victorian Reviewers at Work', *Victorian Periodicals Newsletter* IX (September 1976), 83–7.
32. BL Add. MSS 34615, f.362.
33. Morley, p.272.
34. BL Add. MSS 34616, f.7; *Henry Crabb Robinson on Books and their Writers*, ed. Edith J. Morley, 3 vols (London: Dent, 1938), I, 398.
35. BL Add. MSS 34614, f.615.
36. *Napier*, p.151.
37. Lockhart–Croker Correspondence, *Notes and Queries*, 18 November 1944.
38. *Notes and Queries*, 23 March 1946.
39. See Scott, *Journal*, II, 143; Scott, *Letters*, X, 196, 323.
40. Lockhart–Croker Correspondence, *Notes and Queries*, 23 March 1946
41. George Paston, *At John Murray's: Records of a Literary Circle 1843–1892* (London: John Murray, 1932), p.8; *Henry Crabb Robinson on Books and their Writers*, ed. Morley, II, 541.
42. For an account of the *Westminster*'s precarious finances, see Sheila Rosenberg, 'The Financing of Radical Opinion: John Chapman and the *Westminster Review*' in Joanne Shattock and Michael Wolff, ed. *The Victorian Periodical Press: Samplings and Soundings* (Leicester: Leicester University Press, 1982), pp.145–66; for the *Foreign Quarterly Review* see Eileen M. Curran, 'The Foreign Quarterly Review (1827–1846): a British Interpretation of Modern European Literature', unpublished doctoral thesis, Cornell University, 1958.
43. Scott, *Letters*, X, 414, 421.
44. See Appendix for a note on pirated editions of the *Edinburgh* and the *Quarterly*.
45. BL Add. MSS 34617, f.149.
46. Stephen Koss, *The Rise and Fall of the Political Press in Britain*, 2 vols (London: Hamish Hamilton, 1981), I, 25.

47. On the early circulation, see Chapter I, note 20; see also *Edinburgh Review*, CXCVI, 289.
48. Macaulay, *Letters*, I, 257.
49. Andrew Lang, *The Life and Letters of John Gibson Lockhart*, 2 vols (London: John C. Nimmo, 1897), II, 247.
50. 'Lord Jeffrey's *Contributions to the Edinburgh Review*', *North British Review*, I (May 1844), 261.

Chapter 5

THE 'REVIEW-LIKE ESSAY' AND THE 'ESSAY-LIKE REVIEW'

Looking back on their predecessors, the second generation of editors, in charge of periodicals like the *National Review*, the *Cornhill*, and the *Fortnightly*, saw the flowering of the *Edinburgh* and the *Quarterly* as a dazzling, never to be repeated phenomenon which had established a vital role for Reviews and reviewing in the intellectual life of the period. Because of the *Edinburgh* and the *Quarterly*, review writing had become, as Bagehot had said, 'one of the features of modern literature'.[1]

But Bagehot, Leslie Stephen and John Morley in turn professed disappointment in the quality of the reviewing. When viewed in the cold light of day, Bagehot's 'review-like essay' or 'essay-like review', was flimsy, superficial, and essentially ephemeral. It lacked 'that solidity of workmanship which is essential for enduring vitality'[2], as Stephen put it. By implication, things were different in the 1860s and 1870s. There was more literary ability around, and this talent automatically found its way into periodical literature. Most of the reviewing of the past age, it was inferred, would not pass muster in the present system.

Hindsight of course has its own distortions, and it was only to be expected that the legend of the *Edinburgh* and the *Quarterly* would be challenged and scrutinized by the next generation. The original practitioners, both the first and second generation of reviewers, were ambivalent, not to say schizophrenic, about the status of their work. Its ephemeral nature was something that struck them all. A periodical should have immediate success in order to secure so much as existence, James Mill insisted, in his review of 'Periodical Literature' in the first number of the *Westminster* in January 1824:

> A periodical production must be read the next day, or month, or quarter, otherwise it will not be read at all. Every motive, therefore, which prompts to the production of anything periodical, prompts to the study of immediate effect, of unpostponed popularity, of the applause of the moment.[3]

This, for Mill, limited both the *Edinburgh* and the *Quarterly*'s power to change deeply held convictions or entrenched positions. Because their effect was instant, they could only pandar to the prejudices of their readers, and patronize the opinions currently in vogue. They could not afford and had not the ability, in other words, to challenge the status quo. Mill had his own axe to grind about the unsatisfactory politics of the existing quarterlies and his line of attack, particularly on the *Edinburgh*, soon became clear (see Chapter 6). But his point about immediate success underlined the general uncertainty about the nature and status of reviewing. John Stuart Mill echoed his father's doubts in the *Autobiography*, when he commmented that writing for the press could never be a permanent resource for anyone qualified to accomplish anything in 'the higher departments of literature' because 'the writings by which one can live are not the writings which themselves live'.[4]

Macaulay's irritation at the cuts made in his article on 'The Utilitarian Theory of Government' in the October 1829 *Edinburgh* (see above p. 25) was occasioned not by pique at editorial prerogative, but because Napier had cut out 'the most pointed and ornamented' sentences in the review, stylistic embellishment which he considered part and parcel of review writing:

> Now for high and grave works, a history for example, or a system of political or moral philosophy, Doctor Johnson's rule — that every sentence which the writer thinks fine, ought to be struck out, is excellent. But periodical works like ours, which unless they strike at the first reading are not likely to strike at all, — whose whole life is a month or two — may, I think, be allowed to be sometimes even viciously florid. Probably, in estimating the real value of any tinsel which I may put upon my articles, you and I should not materially differ. But it is not by his

own taste, but by the taste of the fish, that the angler is determined in his choice of bait.

His own taste was changing, he told Napier, and he wrote less floridly than he had done some years ago, and in any extensive work he would write less floridly still than he did in the *Edinburgh*. Empson, siding inevitably with Macaulay, expressed surprise that Napier had cut the passages and wondered aloud whether his taste in composition ran more to 'severer and graver' writing, such as was suitable to scientific subjects and to more 'substantial' works, such as the *Encyclopædia Britannica*, he might have added. Napier did not make sufficient allowance for 'the popular excitements to which the public's palate has been accustomed'.[5]

This sense that periodical writing must be flashy, exaggerated, tinselly — Macaulay's phrase captured the essence of the point — and therefore not substantial enough to withstand the more measured scrutiny of time, was a widespread assumption. Macaulay's comment on Brougham's periodical writings nine years later summarized the position:

> They are indeed models of magazine-writing as distinguished from other sorts of writing. They are not, I think, made for duration. Everything about them is exaggerated, incorrect, sketchy... And the style, though striking and animated, will not bear examination through a single paragraph. But the effect of the first perusal is great, and few people read an article in a Review twice. A bold, dashing, scene-painting manner is that which always succeeds best in periodical writing.[5]

Leslie Stephen concurred in this estimate of Brougham's journalism. All his work was essentially ephemeral, 'a forcible exposition of the arguments common at the time; but... nowhere that stamp of originality in thought or brilliance in expression which could confer upon it a permanent vitality'.[6]

It would seem then that there was 'literature' and 'periodical literature'. Macaulay was the most persistent advocate of the dichotomy. Napier's objections to some of his more colloquial phrasing in his essay on Frederick the Great (April 1842) prompted yet another explication:

> I certainly should not, in regular history, use some of the phrases which you censure. But I do not consider a review of this sort as regular history... Take Addison, the model of pure and graceful writing. In his

Spectators, I find 'wench', 'baggage', 'queer old put', 'prig', 'fearing they should smoke the Knight'... I would no more use the words *bore* or *awkward squad* in a composition meant to be uniformly serious and earnest than Addison would, in a state paper, have called Louis an old put, or have described Shrewsbury and Argyle as smoking the design to bring in the Pretender.

His approach to reviewing assumed that this sort of composition had its own character and its own laws. Where the subject merited it, 'historical articles may rise, if the author can manage it, to the highest altitudes of Thucydides. Then again, they may without impropriety sink to the levity and colloquial ease of Horace Walpole's Letters. This is my theory.' He never thought of denying that the language of history ought to preserve a certain dignity. 'I would, however no more attempt to preserve that dignity in a paper like this on Frederick, than I would exclude from such a poem as Don Juan slang terms because such terms would be out of place in Paradise Lost, or hudibrastic rhymes because such rhymes would be shocking in Pope's Iliad.'[7]

There was then history proper and historical writing suitable for periodicals, Thucydides as opposed to Horace Walpole. The sense that periodical writing was a thing apart from serious literature was a view to which virtually all of this generation of reviewers subscribed. Even Carlyle, who had less reason than many to make the distinction, was resentful of the fact that well-paid work for the *Edinburgh* had kept him from his more serious tasks, lamenting to Napier early in 1831 that he had 'idled of late too long' at 'essay-work'.[8]

The question of status came to a head with the issue of republication, something which did not seriously present itself until the late 1830s. Editors instinctively disliked collections of reprinted essays, fearing that they might cut into the sales of back numbers. On the other hand, it was not unknown for editors to reprint successful single numbers containing a particularly important article. However, the reprintings were almost always occasioned by political or at least topical articles rather than by outstanding essays on literature or other subjects. And given the frenetic nature of most reviewing, few reviewers had the time or inclination to take stock of their output, let alone to consider whether these hastily assembled, supposedly ephemeral productions, were worthy of collection and republication.

Macaulay's *Essays* provided a test case. From the beginning he had opposed republication for the reasons implicit in his discussions on periodical style, as he again summarized them to Napier:

The public judges and ought to judge indulgently of periodical works. They are not expected to be highly finished. Their natural life is only six weeks. Sometimes the writer is at a distance from the books to which he wants to refer. Sometimes he is forced to hurry through his task in order to catch the post. He may blunder; he may contradict himself; he may break off in the middle of a story; he may give an immoderate extension to one part of his subject and dismiss an equally important part in a few words. All this is readily forgiven if there be a certain spirit and vivacity in his style. But as soon as he republishes, he challenges a comparison with all the most symmetrical and polished of human compositions.[9]

His reviews, he admitted, were generally thought to be better written, and they certainly lived longer, than the reviews of most other people. This in itself ought to content him. The moment he came forward to demand higher rank, he must expect to be judged by a more severe standard. He had been chastened, he added, by the example of Albany Fonblanque's collected *Examiner* articles *England under Seven Administrations* (1837), which, when published, were compared, not with articles in the *Courier*, the *Globe* or the *Standard* as previously, but with Burke's pamphlets, Pascal's letters and issues of Addison's *Spectator* and *Freeholders*, and had been found wanting.

All of this was of course wonderfully high-minded, but it made little sense in publishers' terms. Longman had been urging republication since 1839. The pressure came from America where a pirated two volume edition had been published in Boston in 1840, a second, by Carey and Hart of Philadelphia in 1841 and a third edition in 1842. Most of the pirated editions, which were regularly smuggled into England, contained errors, 'trash of which I am perfectly guiltless',[10] and the urge to produce an accurate text was the only one which weighed with Macaulay. But in spite of this, in 1842 he decided yet again not to republish.

Napier agreed, again thinking of his sales of back numbers. But by December the threat of an influx of American 'editions' seemed a likely possibility. As part of the near mania to secure copies of the essays, people were reported to be cutting up old numbers of the Review containing Macaulay's articles, and rebinding them. It seemed absurdly dog-in-the-mangerish, as he put it, to take legal steps to keep the American illegal reprints out and not to publish an English edition.[11]

The *Essays* eventually appeared in 1843. Their phenomenal success then and in the ensuing decades more than justified Longman's commercial instinct. Even Macaulay was reluctantly drawn to the conclusion that the hastily constructed essays might have some permanent value after all. Once the decision to republish was taken, Trevelyan noted that he consciously prepared for republication by footnoting various details of which he was critical in the work under review so as not to interrupt the flow of his narrative in the main body of the essay. The essay on Addison was the first to embody the new technique, but as it had also been one of the last articles he published in the *Edinburgh* there was no real opportunity to test the procedure.[12] The earlier essays were republished with almost no emendations, as they had appeared in the Review.

After Macaulay's *Essays* came four volumes of Jeffrey's *Contributions to the Edinburgh Review* in 1844, a superfluous gesture as far as Macaulay was concerned, for he claimed to have read them and re-read them until he knew them by heart.[13] But for the general public, it was an opportunity not just to reminisce, but to acknowledge the size as well as the substance of Jeffrey's contribution to the Review. More importantly, it was a tangible manifestation of the review-like essay and the essay-like review as literature.

Three volumes of Brougham's *Contributions to the Edinburgh Review* followed in 1856, in addition to the first three volumes of his *Collected Works* (1855–61) which had also contained *Edinburgh* material. Southey's *Essays Moral and Political*, including articles from the *Quarterly*, had appeared in two volumes in 1832. Sydney Smith's *Works*, containing some of his *Edinburgh* contributions had been published in 1839 and his *Essays reprinted from the Edinburgh 1802–1818* appeared in 1874. As early as 1835, Murray had proposed a collected edition of Croker's works, of which the *Quarterly* articles were then estimated to form four volumes, but Croker pronounced himself indifferent.[14]

On the one hand, each collection, by its very appearance, reinforced the non-ephemerality of reviewing. On the other, republication provided an opportunity for reassessment and retrospect, and prompted the complacent conclusions of Bagehot, Stephen and Morley that reviewers and reviewing had greatly improved since the old days. Either way, though, quarterly reviewing had shown itself to be more than a six-week wonder.

Bagehot's description of the prototype *Edinburgh* article as 'the review-like essay and the essay-like review' neatly summed up two approaches to reviewing. For Bagehot, reviews had sprung up in answer to a modern need — the easy dissemination of information and opinion in a busy world which left no time for scholarly rumination or wide reading. The modern man needed and wanted to be told what to think on a variety of subjects. The 'essay-like criticism of modern times' was about the length that he liked. The *Edinburgh*, which had begun the system, could be said to be 'the commencement on large topics of suitable views for sensible persons'. Or, as Newman had commented in one of his sermons: 'Most men in this country like opinions to be brought to them, rather than to be at the pains to go out and seek for them'. Hence the extreme influence of periodical publications in that they 'teach the multitude of men what to think and what to say'.[15]

The difference between an essay and a review was never articulated by reviewers or editors, but it is clear from correspondence that most reviewers considered themselves to be writing either one or the other. Inexperienced contributors often began by offering a 'review' of a particular work, a sustained attempt to criticize and explicate. The more experienced tended to choose a subject rather than a book, and then to fasten a title, recent or otherwise, as a heading, or 'peg' as it was generally known, on which to 'hang' the review, in order to give the impression that the essay was in fact a review.

The old style of reviewing as begun in late eighteenth century Reviews like the *Critical*, the *British* and the *Monthly*, consisted of large amounts of material extracted from the books under scrutiny, in order to give a fair indication of its nature and quality. Abused, the system could produce a mere scissors and paste effort, with lengthy, loosely connected extracts accompanied by bland general comments. The use of extracts persisted well into the next century, cherished by those who had grown up in the old school. Croker, for one, regularly used them, and liberally, in his reviews, insisting that apt quotation was the best way of letting an author either promote or condemn himself. But his reviews were anything but scissors and paste. It was his view that a reviewer ought to *review*, that a line should be taken, and a point made. Those at the receiving end often had reason to wish that their reviewer had gone in for a more discursive essay or a series of lengthy extracts.

He was passionate, too, about the elimination of dullness in reviewing. Writing to Murray in 1823, while helping Gifford in the last stages of his editorship, he complained violently about a review of Southey's *History of the Peninsular War* which was 'a mere abstracted history of the war itself and not in the least a review of the book'. Lockhart was in total agreement, reinforcing the same point in 1838 in connection with Croker's review of the life of Wilberforce, which he insisted should not be merely an abridged life, but rather 'a *review* — a summary of the reflections to which the study of such a career ought to give birth'.[16]

Occasionally, however, Croker himself abandoned readability altogether in a remorseless pursuit of errors in the unfortunate work under review. No detail was too small for dispute. The result was an article which makes even the densest modern scholarly 'note' a joy to read by comparison. In his fury over the *Edinburgh*'s review of his edition of Lady Suffolk's letters (March 1824) by G. J. W. Agar-Ellis, he set down in corresponding double columns the 'corrected' facts and his own facts together with his sources. This indigestible compilation was printed verbatim in *Blackwood*'s (August 1824).[17]

Croker and Macaulay revelled in interminable jousts over detail in their reviewing. Macaulay, as we have seen, usually confined his discussion of detail to the beginning of his reviews, so as not to interrupt the main flow of narrative. Not so Croker who regularly went in for the kill with a blunderbuss effect. The result was an avalanche of detail from which it was sometimes impossible to retain a sense of the main thread of argument. Even the most irascible modern reviewer would be likely to confine these to a handful in the hope that careful selection would do the most damage, but not Croker. He described his review of Lister's *Life of Clarendon*, which had taken him nearly two months to write, as 'a kind of literary rabbit shooting, in which I ferret out all Lister's small facts & then endeavour to kill them before they can escape into their native obscurity.' Empson wittily described the same review as an example of Croker's 'minute microscopic love of picking up straws', and added that if one were to take him up on each of his points the result would be a work longer than the six-volume life of Clarendon. He advised Lister not to allow the review to annoy him and not to take Croker on at his own game. The general impertinence could be answered in two or three sentences, but the 'minute criticisms are a hedgehog it will never do to pick up'.[18]

By Bagehot's distinction, Croker wrote reviews as opposed to essays, conscious, but not always conscious enough, of the dangers of dilution that too many extracts could produce. His was the less glamorous of the two modes of reviewing. The reviewer was the explicator, the summarizer, the analyst, the critic who detected errors and weaknesses, who pointed out main lines of argument and made conclusions. In its most idealistic form this method presented the critic as a self-effacing servant of literature who drew attention to a new work or author, but who on the whole kept his personality hidden.

The antithesis, the other half of Bagehot's phrase, was the writer of the review-like *essay*. The essayist used the book or books under review as an excuse for a discourse on a subject which interested him. As well as the exhilarating freedom which the essay offered, the opportunities for self-promotion and self-display were a temptation. Egocentricity was a charge which was easy to make against the essayist.

As a reviewing practice, the use of pegs was as time honoured as that of using lengthy extracts. Articles on political and economic issues had never been reviews in any sense. MacCulloch's articles were entirely prompted by issues of the day: the poor law, trade with France, the corn laws, with parliamentary reports, pamphlets and speeches hastily prefixed at the eleventh hour to retain the pretence of reviewing. Brougham cheerfully admitted that his contributions were not 'reviews' at all. They frequently arrived with the heading left blank, followed by instructions for the insertion of a speech or pamphlet in order to conform to the format of the other articles. Two articles for the January 1838 number, one on the Education Bill and another on 'Tests and Toleration' were sent off without headings. Brougham proposed a book off the top of his head for the first, and asked Napier to put in 'any book or tract at all' for the second.[19] In addition to his political articles, however, he did occasionally write others which were closer in concept to a review or a review-essay.

Croker was similarly casual about the headings of his political articles. On one occasion he sent off an article to Murray with the request that he send him 'any peg on which I could decently hang it'. Henry Cockburn, writing on 'Parliamentary Representation of Scotland' in the October 1830 *Edinburgh*, had no book to suggest for a text, but told Napier to select an election pamphlet instead. It was, as William Whewell observed, 'a convenient and blameless practice', provided no false implications were made with regard to the work placed at the head of the article.[20]

Macaulay was generally regarded by all as the essayist-reviewer *par excellence*. From the beginning he made no secret of his delight in the flexibility of the *Edinburgh* format, which enabled him to indulge his interests and also to rely often solely on his memory. Some of his contributions were conceived as straight reviews, for . example Moore's *Life of Lord Byron*, Croker's edition of Boswell, and Southey's edition of Bunyan. But even these, once points of disagreement or special note were dealt with, expanded into idiosyncratic essays on their subjects, and Macaulay's gift for effortless prose took over.

It was more often the case that a book was selected because it offered the opportunity for Macaulay to write on a subject that interested him. Charles Sumner's translation and printing of *De Doctrina Christiana* in 1825 had provided him with possibly the most celebrated of all pegs, and he followed his early practice throughout his career. He told Napier he was considering a review of Lord Mahon's *History of the War of the Succession in Spain* provided that it was 'good enough to deserve a sentence of commendation', as he had a kindness for his lordship and should not like to cut up his work. The nature of the war, he emphasized, would make a capital subject. The previous year he had expressed interest in writing on Hampden, provided a recent book on him, Lord Nugent's *Memorials of John Hampden* could be praised 'with a safe conscience'. Finding, when he read it, that it was 'dreadfully heavy', he confessed he had said as little about it as he possibly could. On another occasion he requested a copy of a recent life of Lord Burghley by Edward Nares, which he said would serve as a heading for an article on the times of Elizabeth, no matter how bad the book might be. A life of Pitt by Francis Thackeray published in 1827 was used as a heading for an article in January 1834, with Macaulay arguing that as it had received very little notice when it was published there was no reason for not having an article on it now. The essay on Bacon was ostensibly a review of Basil Montague's *Life of Lord Bacon*, but when it threatened to occupy more than a hundred pages, even he wondered if it were not too long for an article in a periodical. It could not, under any circumstances, have been described as a review of Montague, but rather represented the fruits of extensive reading and reflection over several years.[21]

For Macaulay, Napier and the *Edinburgh* provided a congenial atmosphere in which to try to balance literature and politics, the dichotomy which had become so central to his life in the 1830s and early 1840s. But after India the *History* and his enhanced political responsibilities pushed reviewing into a peripheral role. True to his word however the essays kept coming, on Sir William Temple (October 1838), on Gladstone's *Church and State* (April 1839), on

Clive (January 1840), on Ranke's *History of the Popes* (January 1841), 'Comic Dramatists of the Restoration' ((January 1841), Lord Holland (July 1841), Warren Hastings (October 1841), Frederic the Great (April 1842), and finally on Madame d'Arblay (January 1843), the last essay prior to the publication of the collected edition later that year.

His talents were perfectly suited to review writing. His prodigious memory, his vast store of knowledge and the speed at which he worked had made the *Edinburgh* a useful and not too demanding training ground for the *History*. It also made the literary reputation which the *History* eventually crowned. And more immediately the *Edinburgh* articles brought him to the notice of the Whigs, one of whom rewarded him with a seat in Parliament.

In his biography of Lockhart Andrew Lang contrasted Macaulay and Lockhart, these two prolific reviewers of the same literary generation, the one, initially made famous by his articles in the *Edinburgh Review*, the other, more prolific by far, whose reputation as a reviewer evaporated instantly, and who was remembered as the author of some minor novels and as the biographer of Scott. Lockhart's theory of reviewing, according to Lang, was deliberately self-effacing. He knowingly sacrificed permanence, in order to undertake what he regarded as 'a humble and trivial function':

> He is not the independent essayist, who treats his author only as a starting-point for a tractate of his own; he is merely the journalist, merely the newsman of letters. His duties are of the day and the hour; his business is with his author, and with his author's treatment of a topic, rather than with the topic itself. We may lament this conscious self-effacement; we may and do, regret that Lockhart did not adopt the method of Macaulay and of Carlyle. But he deliberately eschewed it; to do so was part of a character which as a friend of his remarked, detested to 'show off' or to be 'shown off'.

Lang then quoted Lockhart himself on the role of the reviewer:

> We adhere to our old fashioned notion, that, when a man of rich endowments makes his first appearance, or offers the first specimen of what seems to be the main monument of his literary energy ... it is the primary duty of reviewers to think not of themselves but of their author; to put the rein on indulgence in any sort of display except the display of his qualities; to aim, in short, at encouraging his zeal by awakening the curiosity and sympathy of his and their public... This excludes all chance of formal, original, or would-be original disquisition on the part of the journalist.

It was a nice bit of special pleading — Lockhart unselfishly opting for mediocrity and ephemerality when immortality could have been his. It would be nice to think that Lang had a point, were it not for the fact that in reading Lockhart's reviews, one has little sense of a talent held in check, or of a genius for essay writing which he subverted, in order to let a subject speak for itself in a well-chosen extract. He confessed to Croker after finishing the *Life of Scott* that he found the role of the reviewer easier than that of author, 'and a deal more safe as well as dignified'.[22].

We may and do regret, Lang suggested, that Lockhart did not adopt the method of Macaulay and Carlyle. Perhaps even more than Macaulay, Carlyle was the model essayist-reviewer. Probably the most original mind to turn itself to reviewing in the late 1820s and 1830s, his commitment to periodicals was a reluctant one from the beginning. His instincts were decidedly those of an essayist rather than a reviewer. But even the essay format imposed limitations on his intellectual activity which he found irksome. A letter to Napier in September 1831, proposing an article on Moore's *Life of Byron*, illustrated the problem:

> 'tho no Whig in the strict sense, I have no disposition to run *amuck* against any set of men or of opinions, but only to put forth certain Truths that I feel in me, with all sincerity; for some of which this *Byron*, if you liked it, were a fit enough channel. Dilettantism and mere toying with Truth, is, on the whole a thing which I cannot practise; nevertheless real Love, real Belief, is not inconsistent with Tolerance of its opposite; nay is the only thing consistent therewith, for your Elegant Indifference is at heart only *idle*, selfish and quite *in*tolerant. At all events, one can and should *speak quietly*; loud hysterical vehemence, foaming and hissing least of all beseems him that is convinced, and not only *supposes* but *knows*. So much to cast some faint light for you on my plan of procedure and what you have to look for in employing me.[23]

Poor prosaic Napier, 'Naso the Blockhead', as Carlyle had once called him, must have been relieved to be able to reply that Moore's Byron was spoken for. Carlyle also proposed in turn an Essay on Luther ('the whole matter is still only like a chaos in my own head; but the materials are in my possession or within my reach, neither is the will wanting'); 'a faithful, loving and yet critical and in part condemnatory delineation of Jeremy Bentham and his place and working in this section of the World's History'; and an essay on 'the position of the author in our system of society'.[24] Napier found each new suggestion more worrying than the last, and fumblingly found reasons for refusing them. Their general vagueness apart, none of the suggestions were related to actual publications.

To Napier's credit he proposed that Carlyle review William Taylor's *Historic Survey of German Poetry* (March 1831), and he engineered, albeit unwittingly, the writing of 'Characteristics' (December 1831). He also accepted Carlyle's proposal to review Ebenezer Elliott's *Corn-Law Rhymes* (July 1832). His troubled relationship with his gifted contributor, whose gifts he only partially recognized, was governed by his own instinctive caution, and also by the less than enthusiastic response of his colleagues, as we have seen in Chapter 2. But the real problem lay with Carlyle himself. The task of writing an essay, let alone a review, was like trying to bottle an expanding gas. He chafed against the necessity of writing for periodicals. 'Living here by Literature is either serving the Devil or fighting against him at fearful odds,' he told his brother.[25]

Yet offers 'in the literary Periodical way' were coming thick and fast. 'Two or three magazine men are chirping to me with open arms', he reported to his sister. Bulwer had approached him for the *New Monthly Magazine*. He was in correspondence with William Tait of *Tait's Magazine*. 'Tom' Holcroft, who had published the old *Monthly*, wanted to recruit him. James Fraser pressed him to write for *Fraser's*. Cochrane of the *Foreign Quarterly* had engaged him. 'One has no right vehicle: you must throw your ware into one of those dog's-meat carts, such as travel the public streets and get it sold there,' he told his brother, echoing his earlier allusion to the process of placing one's work in periodicals.[26]

His preference was for the *Edinburgh*. 'There is no Periodical so steady as the *Edinburgh Review*, the salary fair, the vehicle respectable,' he wrote to his brother; 'I have Articles in my head; but if Naso behave himself he shall have the pick of the bunch,' he told John later in the year.[27]

By the time 'Corn-Law Rhymes' appeared, in July 1832, Carlyle had sensed that his association with the Review was coming to an end. He was not altogether sorry. He was anxious to abandon periodicals and to write books, but the system, as he saw it, was against him. He told John Stuart Mill in October:

I had hoped that by and by I might get out of Periodicals altogether, and write Books; but the light I got in London last winter showed me that *this* was as good as over. My Editors of Periodicals are my Booksellers, who (under certain new and singular conditions) purchase and publish my *Books* for me, a monstrous method yet still a method ... A question often suggests itself, whether we shall never have our own Periodical Pulpit, and *exclude* the Philistine therefrom, above all, keep the Pew-opener (or Bibliopolist) in his place; and so preach nothing but the sound word?[28]

He continued to write for the *Foreign Quarterly* and for *Fraser's* which from November 1833 began to serialize 'Sartor Resartus'. A year later, in the autumn of 1834, he began work on the *French Revolution.*

For the next generation of editors and reviewers it was Carlyle who stood out as the giant of the periodical scene of the 1830s, who dominated it, yet resented it, chafed against it, and ultimately withdrew from it. John Morley, in his review of Napier's published correspondence, noted with dismay the rough passage which he was given at the hands of Jeffrey and Napier. Lang, in his biography of Lockhart, described the affectionate friendship between the two men, and traced, with sadness, Lockhart's gradual entanglement with journalism, while Carlyle single-mindedly cut himself free:

> No journalist, by the very nature of his duties, has the undisturbed leisure which literature demands, and Lockhart was a journalist. Mr. Carlyle, during these very years, was occupied with great works, and was building his own literary monument. Readers of Mr. Carlyle's journals can readily imagine what sort of monument he would have erected, had he been obliged eternally to keep an eye on 'the literary movement', to watch the stream of new books, to criticize things in general 'from Poetry to Dry-rot', to be abreast, or a few yards in advance, of novelties in politics, and in matters theological and ecclesiastical and social.[29]

Carlyle's good fortune, or good sense, as Lang saw it, had been to escape the clutches of periodical literature, and to concentrate on his books.

It was a nice irony, that the most original mind associated with periodical literature in the 1830s, whose association helped to dignify the profession of journalism, should have resented his entanglement, and endeavoured to escape from it, and that the one periodical respected by him, and for which he would willingly have continued to write, so seriously undervalued him. The *Edinburgh* was undoubtedly the poorer, could it have seen it, for the loss of Carlyle.

And yet it was perhaps inevitable. He was the one contributor for whom the review-like essay or the essay-like review proved a wholly uncongenial medium.

Sydney Smith's well known quip that he never read a book before reviewing it because it prejudiced a man so[30] suggested a pose of irresponsibility among the reviewing fraternity that was by no means universal. On the whole, most reviewers took their work seriously, although most were capable of self-deception both as to the laboriousness and also the speed of their writing. Few had the luxury of an entire working day to devote to the task. For most, reviewing was a supplementary activity, squeezed in before or after other commitments. John Barrow regarded reviewing as welcome relaxation and amusement after his 'dry labours' at the Admiralty, and wrote in the evenings after dinner. In the early thirties, as has been noted, Macaulay regularly rose at five when he had not been speaking in the House and wrote his reviews before breakfast. James Stephen similarly expected to write ten pages for the *Edinburgh* before breakfast and before beginning his day at the Colonial Office.[31]

Brougham told Napier that he had written his March 1831 article on 'Reform and the Ministry', 'exactly as I should have spoken it — extempore'. The analogy was an accurate one as the political articles were often last minute, hastily prepared responses to immediate questions written with the flair of a political orator. The manuscripts of his articles which remain bear this out, page upon page in his execrable long hand with scarcely any alterations or crossings out. He told Napier late in 1835 that he wrote 'far too easily'. The six articles in the April 1835 number had been written at the rate of sixteen pages of print in one day. The two in the October 1835 number had both been written in two evenings and an hour the following morning.[32]

Macaulay too wrote quickly. His correspondence suggests a preparation time of several days per article, increasing to as much as a week or more, all of it sandwiched between his official commitments. He found close textual work irksome and preferred to write from memory. In a particularly busy period in 1838 he confided that he wished he could think of something for the next number that he could write without much reference to books. 'When I write from my own head I go very fast indeed. But when I have to compare a dozen volumes every line that I write, I make but slow work of it,' he told Napier. Trevelyan recalled the change in Macaulay's working methods which occurred when he began serious work on the *History*. He took careful notes from all sources outside his own library, 'instead of continuing the facile, though hazardous course which he had pursued as a Reviewer and trusting to his memory alone'.[33]

Scott also reviewed at speed. His journal from 1827 onwards recorded reviews written in a couple of days or even evenings. There was an added urgency after the crash of 1826, but the sense is that this was a preferred rhythm of working. He was particularly sparing in the time he devoted to reviews for the *Foreign Quarterly* in view of the meagre financial rewards.

Southey and Croker were easily the *Quarterly*'s most professional reviewers. Croker contributed ninety-nine articles to the first hundred numbers of the Review, the bulk of these at a time when he was Secretary to the Admiralty. Like all reviewers who wrote regularly, he could write quickly. Thirty-two pages of his review of the Duke of Wellington's Despatches (June 1834) were written in four hours, yet in 1838, he groaned under what he claimed were the four to six hours a day for five weeks he spent in preparing his review of Lister's *Clarendon*. Like Macaulay he relied on memory a great deal, although the reviews containing copious extracts could not have been done without a close familiarity with the text. His reviews on aspects of the French Revolution on which he was an acknowledged expert were sometimes done without the aid of books. On one occasion, an article on Robespierre was dashed off during a holiday at the seaside, and then checked when he returned to his library.[34]

Southey's main source of income was his work for the *Quarterly*. 'Literature is now Southey's trade,' Crabb Robinson had noted in his Diary; 'He is a manufacturer, and his study is his workshop... His time is his wealth; and I shall therefore scrupulously abstain from stealing any portion of it.'[35] Southey told his protégé J. T. Coleridge that reviewing was his most profitable line of composition and that he had not yet received as much for his *History of the Brazils* as he had from a single article in the *Quarterly*. His ability to 'tear the heart out of a book' was one of the legends of reviewing. According to Samuel Smiles he was able to glance rapidly through a book, sticking in notes as markers, and, with the use of his remarkable memory, within a few hours could have enough materials for an interesting paper, one which offered a complete analysis of its subject and not just a series of extracts. According to Smiles, Southey could easily have filled a whole number himself.[36]

Not all reviewers had the facility for fast work, and even the most experienced did not work at breakneck speed all the time. MacCulloch claimed to have had the skeleton of his article on property and income tax (April 1833) burdening him for over two years and to have written every word of it twice over and some of it three times. Macaulay told Napier that nothing he had ever written had cost him a quarter of the labour he had put into the latter part of his essay on Bacon. Carlyle rarely took less than a month over his reviews and usually longer, which was no doubt why he chafed against the need to review regularly. The review of Taylor's *Historic Survey of German Poetry* took him a month, and 'Characteristics', when he eventually defined the subject, took almost two.[37]

Inexperienced reviewers inevitably took longer over their articles. Sir John Herschel, according to Lockhart, spent all winter on his review of Whewell's *History of the Inductive Sciences* (June 1841). Thomas Flower Ellis offered a review of Palgrave's *Merchant and Friar* but told Napier it would take him six weeks and more probably two months. He actually completed it in one. R. B. Hampton, a prospective reviewer, was flattered at Napier's suggestion that he write on Plato, but felt he could not produce anything in less than three months and in the end, did not produce it at all. James Spedding took upwards of two months to write his first article for the *Edinburgh* and although flattered to be asked, claimed that it hung about him 'like a nightmare'.[38]

Reviewers customarily applied to the publisher, Longman or Murray, for the loan of books needed for a review. The dispatch of free review copies was unknown. Sometimes the editor or reviewer already had the book in his possession, in which case there was no need to draw on the publisher's stock. But Longman and Murray regularly supplied not only the books named in the heading of the reviews, but background material as well. Murray belonged to a circulating library for this purpose. Old hands like Croker and Brougham assumed that the publisher would provide whatever they needed and did not put themselves out to secure the books independently.[39]

Carlyle found himself 'wonderfully circumstanced' in Craigenputtock for books, 'like an old Hebrew doomed to make Bricks and no straw allowed him'. Napier loaned him the three volumes of Taylor's *Historic Survey of German Poetry* for his March 1831 review. Carlyle impulsively sent them to Goethe at Weimar because the latter needed to consult them, and then embarrassingly had to ask that the cost be deducted from his fee for 'Corn-Law Rhymes'. He had great difficulty in locating Thomas Hope's *Essay on the Origin and Prospect of Man* (1831) which Napier had suggested as the basis for his next review, 'Characteristics', together with Schlegel's *Philosophical Lectures*. He glanced at it in the British Museum, but neither Murray nor Longman could provide a copy, so in the end he wrote the article without recourse to either book, cheerfully admitting that the books themselves occupied only two paragraphs out of a total of some thirty pages. He borrowed Elliott's *Corn-Law Rhymes* from John Stuart Mill for his July 1832 review. In June of 1832 Napier promised him a more reliable source of supply, presumably with Longman's consent, which, had his association with the *Edinburgh* not come to an end, would have aided his work considerably. Only on rare occasions were books used as a method of payment, as in the case of Macaulay's period in India when by arrangement he was sent a selection of recent books in lieu of a fee, as a means of keeping himself up to date while abroad.[40]

Publishers sometimes co-operated with editors and reviewers by despatching advance sheets of new works before the official publication date, in order to secure an early review in the *Edinburgh* or the *Quarterly*. It was not unknown for booksellers actually to defer publication in order to facilitate a review. Croker wrote his review of the *Life of Sir James Mackintosh* (July 1835) from the advance sheets forwarded by Lockhart. Some of the sheets which contained Mackintosh's letters were not included and the section relating to them in the review was added by Lockhart. Macaulay similarly had not seen the final sheets of Mackintosh's *History* when he dispatched his review from India, and like Croker was worried because he had had to write his review from the early sheets. James Stephen in effect sold himself to Napier as the reviewer of the *Life of Wilberforce* (April 1838) by his promise to secure the sheets of a greater part of the work before publication from Robert Wilberforce, one of the joint authors. It proved not such an advantage, as the publishers sent him the work in sections and he was not altogether certain, as he told Napier, that he had not missed parts of it.[41]

There seems to have been no established policy on proofs. The irritation with which Lord Mahon, Poulett Scrope, and Harriet Martineau viewed Croker's handiwork suggests that the *Quarterly* was not in the habit of sending out proofs before publication.

Southey's fulminations against Gifford and Macaulay's fury when a printer's error had caused inadvertent omissions as well as Napier's deliberate cuts similarly suggests that proofs were not a regular procedure in either Review. On the other hand Brougham, with characteristic peremptoriness, frequently requested proofs of his articles within two days and sometimes a second revise. Similarly, Napier's younger recruits, Henry Rich and T. H. Lister prided themselves on the number of ministers to whom they sent proofs of their articles for approval.[42]

The mechanics of the reviewing process apart, the reviewer's lot was a hectic one, and made more so by the fact that few reviewers worked full time at the job. As to what made a good reviewer as opposed to a mediocre one, the answers were as diverse as the reviewers themselves. Bagehot's suggestion that Scottish education was 'designed to teach men to write essays and articles' and that the 'general, diversified, omnipresent information' of the North was superior in this respect to the 'particular, compact, exclusive' learning in England,[43] made a nice debating point, and was helped by the high incidence of translated Scots in the world of letters. But the qualities of a good reviewer had also to be learned, and then not over-worked. T. J. Hogg, struggling under the misapprehension that he was supposed to summarize Niebuhr's *History of Rome* in his review, muttered aloud about 'microscopic penmanship that can bring the Lord's Prayer within the compass of a pea',[44] a dubious talent, by anyone's reckoning. Reviewing was a craft, and practice helped.

But Lang's admittedly partisan portrait of Lockhart as reviewer, consciously self-effacing, in order to do his duty to the author, but more to the point, worn down by the sheer volume of the job, forced to criticize everything 'from poetry to dry-rot', and then to keep abreast of politics, theology, and social matters, presented the reviewer's dilemma with stark clarity. Success went almost entirely to those who set their sights higher, who regarded the quarterlies as a training ground or, in Carlyle's case, a source of income, but who aimed at the world of 'Books', or 'Literature' proper rather than devoting themselves exclusively to journalism. The ideal situation was the one which the editors in the 1860s and 1870s thought they had achieved, in which there was a fluid relationship between the periodicals and the larger literary world, in which, as Leslie Stephen insisted, 'much of the most solid and original work of the time' appeared first in periodicals.[45]

Southey constructing his reviews with practised efficiency, Croker pursuing his prey to the death, leaving no detail unturned, Macaulay juggling the *History*, active politics and reviewing at a breathless pace, and Carlyle smouldering resentfully under Napier's neglect, producing 'Characteristics' in the teeth of the opposition, not caring in the end whether it was published or not — each in his way was a typical quarterly reviewer, and each contributed, not insignificantly, to the status and the influence of the form.

Notes

1. Bagehot, 'The First Edinburgh Reviewers', *Literary Studies*, I, 2.
2. Stephen, 'The First Edinburgh Reviewers', *Hours in a Library*, II, 269.
3. [James and J.S. Mill], 'Periodical Literature: Edinburgh Review', *Westminster Review*, I (January 1824), 207.
4. John Stuart Mill, *Autobiography*, p.85.
5. Macaulay, *Letters*, I, 261, III, 250; Napier Correspondence, BL Add. MSS. 34614, f.251.
6. Stephen, *Hours in a Library*, II, 252–3.
7. Macaulay, *Letters*, IV, 27–8.
8. BL Add. MSS. 34615, f.33.
9. Macaulay, *Letters*, IV, 40–1
10. Macaulay, *Letters*, IV, 40.
11. Macaulay, *Letters*, IV, 79.
12. G. O. Trevelyan, *Life and Letters of Lord Macaulay*, 2 vols (London, 1876), II, 125, 129n.
13. Trevelyan, II, 128.
14. Samuel Smiles, *A Publisher and his Friends: Memoir of John Murray*, 2 vols (London: John Murray, 1891), II, 380.
15. Bagehot, *Literary Studies*, I, 6; 'Christ upon the Waters' (1850), *Sermons Preached on Various Occasions* (London, 1898), pp.148–9, quoted by W. E. Houghton, *The Victorian Frame of Mind* (New Haven: Yale University Press, 1957), p.104. In the preface to *The Idea of a University*, Newman remarked that the modern journalist lay under 'the stern obligation of extemporizing his lucid views, leading ideas, and nutshell truths for the breakfast table'. *The Idea of a University*, ed. I. T. Ker (Oxford: Clarendon Press, 1976), p.13.
16. Samuel Smiles, *A Publisher and His Friends: Memoir and Correspondence of John Murray*, 2 vols (London: John Murray, 1897), II, 57; Lockhart–Croker Correspondence, *Notes and Queries*, 9 September 1944.
17. See Croker to Lockhart, 4 August 1824, quoted by Lott, pp.58–60.
18. Croker to Lockhart, 14 September 1838, quoted by Davis, p.65; BL

Add MSS. 34619, ff.455, 476.

19. BL Add. MSS. 34617, f.125; 34,618, f.478.
20. Croker to Murray, 25 January 1837, Murray Papers; BL Add. MSS. 34 614, f.410; 34617, f.305.
21. Macaulay, *Letters*, II, 190, 108, 110–11, 316; III, 163.
22. Andrew Lang, *The Life and Letters of John Gibson Lockhart*, 2 vols (London: John C. Nimmo, 1897), II, 257–8; Lockhart–Croker Correspondence, *Notes and Queries*, 9 September 1944.
23. Carlyle, *Letters*, V, 196.
24. Carlyle, *Letters*, V, 403, 211.
25. Carlyle, *Letters*, VI, 71.
26. Carlyle, *Letters*, VI, 79, 85. (See also infra, p.3)
27. Carlyle, *Letters*, V, 213; VI, 71–2.
28. Carlyle, *Letters*, VI, 241.
29. Lang, II, 246.
30. Quoted in Hesketh Pearson, *The Smith of Smiths* (London, 1934), p.54.
31. John Barrow, *An Auto-biographical Memoir of Sir John Barrow* (London: John Murray, 1847), p.502; on Stephen's reviewing, see DNB.
32. BL Add. MSS 34615, f.80; *Napier*, pp.105, 161, 168. Brougham's remaining manuscript articles are in BL Add. MSS. 34627–8.
33. Macaulay, *Letters*, III, 256; Trevelyan, II, 223.
34. Smiles, II, 379; Croker to John Murray III, 5 Sept. 1838, Murray Papers; Croker Papers, II, 283.
35. *Henry Crabb Robinson on Books and their Writers*, ed. Edith J. Morley, 3 vols (London: Dent, 1938), II, 22.
36. Smiles, II, 40.
37. BL Add. MSS. 34616, f.60; Macaulay, *Letters*, III, 195–7; Carlyle, *Letters*, V, 210 n.1, VI, 13.
38. Lockhart–Croker Correspondence, *Notes and Queries*, 9 September 1844; BL Add. MSS. 34618, ff.423, 347, 340.
39. Croker to Lockhart, 9 January 1835, in Davis, p.38; See also for example, M. J. Shiel, who typically wrote to Napier, 'in case I should want any books... will you have the goodness to mention it to Messrs. Longman & Co. that I have your authority for applying for the loan of them', BL Add. MSS. 34615, f. 113.
40. *Napier*, pp.125, 141, 143; Carlyle, *Letters*, V, 420n.23; VI, 13, 177.
41. Croker to Murray, May 1835, Murray Papers; Lockhart to Croker, 1 April 1835, in Lott, p.163; *Napier*, pp.154–5; BL Add. MSS. 34618, ff.440, 631;
42. Thomas Flower Ellis, no doubt exercising beginners' caution, requested a revise of his Palgrave article, BL Add. MSS. 34618, f.425.
43. Bagehot, *Literary Studies*, I, 24–5.
44. *Edinburgh Review*, LI (July 1830), 359.
45. Stephen, *Hours in a Library*, II, 269.

Chapter 6

POLITICS AND REVIEWING IN THE 1830s

Jeffrey's much quoted comment, made to Scott in 1808, that the *Edinburgh Review* had 'but two legs to stand on, literature no doubt is one of them, but its Right leg is politics',[1] nicely articulated the conjunction that was essential to his editorship, and to the *Edinburgh* throughout much of its long history. The combination of political conviction and critical acumen was crucial to the Review, and the leg analogy was accurate — each limb of equal importance, mutually supportive and yet exercising a degree of independence. In practice, the relationship was more problematical and called for a delicate balance, which was not all that easily maintained.

For John Morley, as we have seen, it was the force of shared political conviction that was the essence of the *Edinburgh*'s success. Walter Bagehot and Leslie Stephen, too, noted the role which Whiggish principles and ultimately Whig government played in the development of the *Edinburgh* up to the end of the 1830s. The initial challenge to the *Edinburgh* by the *Quarterly* had been made on political grounds. The real reason for its establishment, as Scott reminded Gifford in 1808, was 'the disgusting and deleterious doctrine with which the most popular of these periodical works disgraces its pages', by which he meant the *Edinburgh*'s politics. And yet, he argued, it would not be advisable that the new quarterly should at the beginning have 'exclusively a political character'.[2] He meant, in this instance, a party political character. In a letter to George Ellis, another *Quarterly* supporter, in December 1808, Scott reported that 'Jeffrey has offered terms of pacification, engaging that no party politics should again appear in his Review. I told him I thought it was now too late, and reminded him that I had often pointed out to him the consequences of letting his work become a party tool.'[3]

Both of these letters were republished by Lockhart as part of the narrative of the founding of the *Quarterly* in the second volume of his *Life of Scott* in 1837. Even after more than thirty years Jeffrey was stung into making a clarification when preparing the introduction to his collected *Edinburgh* articles in 1844. He could never have promised Scott that the *Edinburgh Review* would eschew party politics: 'I have repeatedly told him that, with the political influence we have already acquired, this was not to be expected, and that by such a course the authority of the Review would be fatally impaired, even for its literary judgments.' The misunderstanding occurred, he thought, from Scott's mistaking a desire to avoid *violent* politics for a pledge to avoid all politics: 'As to renouncing politics altogether, or party politics (which in a periodical paper is the same thing), the notion is palpably ridiculous.'[4] The authority of the Review as a whole, Jeffrey implied, was bound up with its political authority. If this were removed, the results would be fatal for its criticism generally.

For the intelligent reading public, there was no doubt about the political nature of the two major Reviews. In a review of 'Periodical Literature' in the first two numbers of the *Westminster* (January and April 1824), James and John Stuart Mill issued a direct challenge to the *Edinburgh* and by implication the *Quarterly*, a challenge based on the premise that they were political reviews. They represented, according to James Mill, opposing sides of the 'aristocracy', his term for the small proportion of society which ultimately held the reins of government. The *Edinburgh* represented the 'Opposition' party of the aristocracy, the Whigs; the *Quarterly*, the Ministerial party, or the Tories. Mill's main point was that neither party nor Review sought radical change in society. Instead they, or rather the *Edinburgh*, which was his main target, followed a policy of compromise, of 'see-saw', of seeking the middle ground, which in effect was to propose nothing which would substantially alter the status quo.

The two articles, the first by the elder Mill, and the second by J. S. Mill, were a blistering and wide-ranging attack on the policies and attitudes of the early *Edinburgh*, and an open declaration of war on the older Reviews by the youngest. It was a challenge which was taken up five years later by Macaulay in a celebrated debate with the *Westminster*.

Ideological rivalry apart, the Mills' articles were important in two other respects. James Mill had raised the question of periodicity, of the nature of periodical literature, which, he argued, had an instant effect, and therefore was condemned to pandar to popular prejudices, the opinions of the moment, the views of those in power. It could not wait for 'that success which depends upon the slow progress of just opinions, and the slow removal of prevalent errors' (Vol.I, 210). Just how the *Westminster* proposed to effect a revolution when it laboured under the same disadvantage was not clear, but Mill's observations on the immediacy and the ephemerality of periodical literature were interesting, and struck a chord with other reflections and anxieties about the nature of the form.

The articles were significant, too, because of the underlying assumption, which was never questioned, that the *Edinburgh* and the *Quarterly* were first and foremost *political* Reviews. James Mill did acknowledge that politics was not the only element in the *Edinburgh*, and that in its treatment of poetry, mathematics, chemistry and other subjects the quality of the reviewing was entirely dependent upon the quality of the individual reviewers, and took no bias from the political affiliations. Indeed, J. S. Mill suggested that in its treatment of some of these areas it allowed itself a tincture of radical or 'advanced' opinion almost to salve its collective conscience over the spirit of compromise and reaction which governed its views on political and social questions.

But in the mind of the newest arrival on the reviewing scene, there was no doubt whatsoever that the senior quarterlies were profoundly affected and indeed directed by political considerations. And in the minds of their editors and reviewers there was no real doubt of this either.

Yet, having accepted that politics was an essential ingredient, the conductors of both the *Edinburgh* and the *Quarterly* were ambivalent, to say the least, about their political commitments. This was particularly true of the *Quarterly*. 'I have strongly advised that politics be avoided, unless in cases of great national import... the general tone of the publication is to be literary,' Scott wrote to another friend. Even Croker was disingenuous about his role in the politics of the *Quarterly* prior to 1830:

> Murray well knows that I never was a friend to making the *Review* a political engine; for twenty years that I wrote in it — from 1809 to 1829 — I never gave, I believe, one purely political article; not one, certainly, in which *party politics* predominated. Nor, even latterly, did I, of my own free will, write political articles. I did what I was desired to do; and what I was told was advantageous to the *Review*... To yourself I have more than once hinted that neither *politics* nor *trifles* can make a sufficient substratum and foundation — *solid literature and science* must be the substance — the rest is 'leather and prunella'. In short, a review should be a *review* and a review of the *higher* order of literature than the ordinary run of the topics and publications of the idle day.[5]

The distinction between 'politics' and 'party politics', it would seem, proved a useful piece of double talk on more than one occasion, but as Jeffrey recognized, they were really the same thing. What both the *Edinburgh* and the *Quarterly* were wary of copying were the links between newspapers and political parties, a relationship in which the papers became crude party organs, the virtual mouthpieces of their sponsors. The quarterlies wanted close links and exclusive sources without strings. And they wanted to be organs of opinion in a general sense, authoritative in many areas, not just in politics. Hence Jeffrey's two legs of the *Edinburgh* and Scott and Croker's repeated insistence that the general tone of the *Quarterly* was to be 'literary'. Further, they sought a status which was greatly superior to the somewhat tawdry image of the newspaper press prior to the 1840s.

On all these counts, they were successful. Louis Jennings, editor of the *Croker Papers*, was accurate when he described the political role of the quarterlies in the early days:

> It frequently happened that news of the gravest importance was first made known to the country through the medium of the political article in the *Edinburgh* or *Quarterly Reviews*. Almost always that article was founded upon intelligence which had been communicated by the heads of the Ministry, or by the originators of some measure which was soon to become the universal theme of discussion. It is evident from Mr. Croker's correspondence that he went for the foundation of many of his essays to the men who alone could rightly know all the facts with which he had to

deal, and thus in many cases, an almost complete draft of the political article was supplied by the Duke of Wellington, by Sir Robert Peel or by some authority of equal weight on the question of the day.[6]

Jennings was referring to the first two decades of the quarterlies' existence, or the period prior to 1830, but some of the direct links and access to government sources were carried over into the next generation.

In November 1830 the relative positions of the *Edinburgh* and the *Quarterly* were dramatically reversed. After nearly thirty years as an opposition journal, the *Edinburgh* became a ministerial review with varying degrees of access to government, and the *Quarterly* declined into what must have seemed the unthinkable position of an opposition journal. Croker's retirement from active politics in 1832 also heralded a change. He still had his contacts, but they counted for less. It was not unknown for a number of the *Quarterly* in the 1830s to appear without a political article, something which rarely happened in the *Edinburgh*. It was the *Edinburgh* which, politically, achieved preeminence in the 1830s. It had become as Carlyle put it flatteringly to Napier, a Review 'now almost demi-official'.[7]

In 1836 Bulwer Lytton wistfully expressed the wish that as a mere 'prose fictionist', he could be entrusted with a political article, but agreed that there were problems about this, and that he knew 'the wheels within wheels by which great Party journals must be worked'.[8] Napier could not have put it more aptly. His correspondence was filled with gossip, rumour and speculation, the heady atmosphere which only close connection with government could produce. He relied almost entirely on his London-based contributors with political connections for intelligence and for the oiling of wheels. His contributors, in turn, were eager to impress their provincial editor with the high level of their sources.

These were in many cases official and authoritative. 'You may rely on my statements. They all come from the best authority,' MacCulloch breezily assured him when submitting an article on Colonial Policy for the December 1831 number. 'I know what the government intends to do and I approve of their plans,' he had written in February of the same year with reference to an article on Pauperism (March 1831). Prior to his article on the bank charter (January 1833) he breakfasted with the governor who gave him a 'full description of the subject'. His article on the East India Company (January 1831) contained several things not included in the evidence before the committee, but were all founded on 'the best authority to be had in London'.[9]

MacCulloch's terrier-like persistence in presenting his credentials was matched by younger reviewers who were just as keen to score with the new editor. Henry Rich and T. H. Lister, both young reviewers with political ambitions, vied with one another in the number of ministerial names they could drop in various proposals to Napier. Lister offered an article on the East India question at the suggestion of his brother-in-law, Hyde Villiers, Secretary of the Board of Control, who promised him 'all the information he was at liberty to reveal'. Lord Palmerston had given him valuable information for an article on Belgium and Holland (January 1833), he claimed, and he had also shown the paper to Lord Lansdowne. Rich also professed to have the ear of Lord Palmerston to whom he sent proofs of his article on Poland (April 1832). Moreover Mr Cutlar Fergusson (a Whig MP and prominent Polish sympathizer) had deferred his motion in the House for several days and would continue to do so until the *Edinburgh* reached London, he told Napier. Rich refused to dispatch his article on Reform Associations (October 1835) until it had the approval of a member of the government. Mr Ellice (formerly Secretary to the Treasury and Secretary at War) had promised to go through it with him, and he would send proofs either to Lord John Russell, or to Spring-Rice, Chancellor of the Exchequer.[10]

Much of this was little more than name-dropping at a rather high level, but close links with government and other official sources did exist. Thomas Spring-Rice, the Chancellor of the Exchequer, was a close associate of the Review and contributed two articles on Ireland (April 1833 and April 1834), which according to Empson were regarded as very helpful to the government. John Ward, a new reviewer writing on the metropolitan police (January 1838), canvassed two of the Criminal Law Commissioners with proofs of the article before publication, but declined to show it to the chairman in case the article appeared to have proceeded directly from the commission. Similarly, Edwin Chadwick offered Napier any inside information which he as a Poor Law Commissioner could supply or information 'on any other subject which comes within my official observation'.[11]

Paradoxically power also produced its own inhibitions. Several of the older contributors now felt themselves disqualified by the extent of their inside knowledge. Henry Cockburn, for example, declined to write an article on Reform in case his authorship might embarrass the government. He felt guilty, he told Napier, about expressing views and opinions which were acquired in confidence. Because of his connections with Holland House, John Allen was unwilling to write an article on political parties, 'least inadvertently I should say more than I ought to communicate', as he put it.[12]

By contrast, the *Quarterly* found itself severely disadvantaged during the same period. Lockhart's lack of political skills and connections troubled Scott among others during the early years of his editorship. The latter's energetic socializing during his visit to London in the autumn of 1826 was an attempt to secure useful contacts. They dined with Croker at the Admiralty, with several Cabinet Ministers including Canning, Peel, Huskisson, Melville and the Duke of Wellington, as well as 'sub-secretaries by the bushel'. Another visit in the spring of 1828 occasioned a similar programme with Scott noting somewhat ruefully: 'I can only tee the ball; he must strike the blow with the golf club himself.'[13]

During the same visit Scott wrote personally to Peel to urge that the government make use of 'a great literary and political engine' under its present loyal editor, and asked whether a 'confidential channel' could be opened between the editor and the government. To Sir William Knighton, the King's private secretary, he hinted that it was not enough for an editor to have a link with a single member of the government:

I must tell you in great confidence that his situation at present a great deal cripples his power of being useful. Members of the government, holding situations of consequence, propose to him articles of the most opposite tendency without his having the means of knowing which with a view to his Majestys [sic] service he ought to prefer. Now if any confidential quarter was pointed out where [a] hint might be given on a question asked it would give energy and efficacy to his interference.

The periodical press, Scott suggested, was of utmost significance:

Men were formerly led by the ears — they are now guided by the eye and the influence of the author has succeeded to that of the orator. The whole daily press seems to me to have embraced democratical opinions without one exception. And it is worth while to secure and effectually direct this very important branch [the quarterlies] of the periodical literature.[14]

No friend or colleague, let alone father-in-law, could have done more to smooth Lockhart's path. But the problem for the *Quarterly*, as Scott well knew, was not just the new editor's political naïvety, but an historical disinclination on the part of the Tory government to utilize the Review. Gifford's moan, years earlier, against 'those Cabinet people who when it is too late... rub their eyes and begin to see that the Review might be of the utmost importance to them but never condescend to write a thought on it,' was finding an echo in the next generation.[15]

The effecting of links between a Review and the government or between a Review and the opposition, was never straightforward. There was always the fear of toadying to be balanced against the fruits of inside information and the privileges of confidentiality. While recognizing the benefits to be derived from the periodical press, governments and political parties seemed reluctant or puzzled as to how best to exploit this particular resource. Gifford's and then Lockhart's difficulties with Tory governments were mirrored by Napier's later difficulty with Melbourne's second administration.

'Information' and 'points of fact' as opposed to 'news' were keywords in quarterly circles. Theirs was to be the long view, the measured judgement, the informed opinion. They wanted nothing to do with newsmongering, or anything with a whiff of sensation. Rehearsing the arguments for a quarterly over other forms of periodical publication in 1808, Scott had argued that greater frequency would not allow sufficient time to collect valuable materials, nor were there sufficient important books to justify more numbers. Neither of these conditions was true in the 1830s. The explosion of publications on all fronts produced a need for careful selection of books. There were too many to review, rather than too few. And the time factor was no longer relevant, for although they stood by their determination not to supply merely news, the quarterlies were as much under the dictation of events as any other periodical form.

The passage of the Reform Bill dominated the political articles of both Reviews from early 1831 onward. 'You ought not — indeed you must not expect us to think or even dream of ought but *Reform* at this crisis,' Empson warned Napier in the weeks leading up to the second reading of the Bill on 22 March 1831. During the same period MacCulloch stressed that the *Edinburgh*'s political articles were 'severely scrutinized' because of Brougham's known connections with the Review. Empson urged the need for balance and caution. 'We want clever writers... a single injudicious or unprincipled or wrong principled article... wd do us more harm than a hundred dull papers,' he reportedly told a new reviewer. Napier should advise him that they wrote for 'prudent & perhaps timid as well as for imaginative politicians'.[16]

Balance and caution were not easy to achieve with Brougham at the helm of the Review's political programme. Until he was dropped from Melbourne's second ministry in April 1835, the Lord Chancellor capitalized ruthlessly on his position, writing to Napier sometimes twice daily, peremptorily holding up a review for twenty-four or even forty-eight hours until 'new information' was secured, or a particular debate had finished, cavalierly announcing that an article would be half as long again as he had previously said, or demanding a second revise so that additional material could be added.

The conduct of the *Quarterly* was similarly frenetic, although relations between Lockhart and Croker were much less stressful than between Napier and Brougham. 'We must now have a short pithy Epilogue on the state of affairs say at the end of next week, for I presume the fate of the Govt. must by that time be determined', Lockhart wrote characteristically in April 1835. 'I don't see that you can have anything to say that wd. do good to the Parliamentary Conservatives for this session,' he wrote prior to the April 1836 number; 'But if you have any reason to think that the conduct of the H. of Lords is as yet unfixed & that you cd. help in the smallest degree to fix it in the right direction, I shall... be only too happy to receive further news.' In August 1838 Lockhart wrote to Murray: 'We have now everything for a first rate No. of [the] Q.R. *except* what Mr. C. alone can give – a first rate political paper showing how & why the govt has fallen in public opinion.' Sheets were regularly sent ahead to the printer to be got ready in case Croker spotted anything on the political scene which prompted a last minute article. The publication date would then depend entirely 'on your convenience & Murray's pleasure', as Lockhart put it.[17]

Croker had years of experience as a political reviewer, but after 1832 his official retirement meant that contacts lessened, and with the Tories in opposition rather than government, official sources and high level information were more difficult to secure. Once Brougham began to war against the government which had turned its back on him, the job of maintaining the *Edinburgh*'s political authority also became more difficult. The now ex-Lord Chancellor became the enemy within, eager to oppose the government in the pages of the Review whenever he could seize the opportunity and quick to counsel Napier not to make the *Edinburgh* a party organ, by which he meant a pro-government Review. When Empson produced an article on the 'State of the Parties' in September 1837, Brougham brusquely informed Napier that none of the ministers approved of it. Empson pointed out that they had more reliable gauges of government approval than Brougham's surmises, and added, rightly, that Brougham would be glad enough to silence the *Edinburgh* as a political organ if he could: 'He is a pretty person truly to advise you & inform you what is useful or agreeable to Ministers in yr. Review.'[18]

The problem of access to information increased, and in the summer of 1837 Napier wrote to Thomas Young, an official close to Melbourne, on the worrying absence of sources. Young replied in confidence that the government, if not blind, were generally 'insouciant' of the advantages to be gained by acting on public opinion through the periodical press. They were guilty of carelessness, 'in not availing themselves of that most powerful instrument — the most potent of any in influencing and directing public opinion & thereby strengthening themselves'. Young also inferred that there was not a lot of inside information to be had: 'It is true that Ld. M. remarked to me that in reality they had not secrets to tell and little information beyond what appeared on the surface'. But if Napier cared to specify points on which he desired directions, Young promised to put the letter before the Prime Minister.[19]

Young proved a useful ally in the final fracas with Brougham, both in the matter of the affront to Melbourne, and in the Wilberforce–Clarkson dispute (see p. 32 *et seq*). He was quick to reassure Napier that the Prime Minister was confident he would resist all future attempts to convert the Review into an instrument of opposition to the government and to the Whig party, a veiled acknowledgement of the trials Napier was by then undergoing at the hands of Brougham. The declared hostility of the *Edinburgh Review* would be an incident of no small importance, Melbourne was reported to have said. Yet despite these reassurances, the *Edinburgh*'s position *vis-à-vis* the Whig government was never quite as secure after 1835 as it had been before.

The three-month interval between issues was long in terms of public attention. The quarterlies had several strategies by which to secure greater publicity, one of the most effective of which was the establishment of a relationship with a newspaper or newspapers. J. A. Stuart, editor of the then Whig *Courier* and an old friend of Napier's was regularly sent the sheets of the *Edinburgh* several days before publication so that a brief article on the forthcoming number could be prepared. MacCulloch, who was a friend of Stuart's, was sometimes given the task of preparing the article and Napier on at least one occasion made him privy to some 'private' details, presumably on authorship, to aid him in the task.

T. H. Lister used all ministerial connections he could muster to see that the *Globe* and the *Morning Chronicle* drew attention to his January 1835 article on the Irish Catholic clergy and the appropriation of church property. After assuring Napier that his subsequent article on the Irish Church in the July number had cabinet approval he suggested that extracts and notices should appear simultaneously in government newspapers. The *Chronicle* did, in the end, notice the article.

Newspapers sometimes of their own accord extracted articles from current numbers of the major quarterlies. Provocative and controversial articles, and extended controversies, were for this reason generally welcomed by editors, provided the issues were neither scurrilous nor libellous, because they brought the Reviews desirable publicity.

Another indication of the wider impact of the quarterlies was the reprinting of specific numbers, usually to satisfy demand for a particular article which had attracted public attention. The April 1838 issue of the *Edinburgh* was reprinted, to Longman's delight, principally because of Brougham's article 'George the Fourth and Queen Caroline — Abuses of the Press', ironic in view of the fact that the article came close to doing considerable damage to the Review's relations with the government (see p. 32). The *Quarterly* regularly reprinted numbers during the 1830s. Murray's ledgers show 250 copies to be the standard reprint, and the issues selected often contained a political article by Croker.

Thinking about his impending return to England during his last year in India, Macaulay commented to Napier that 'the little political squalls which I have had to weather here are mere cap-fulls of wind to a man who has gone through the great hurricanes of English faction'.[20] It was not surprising.

Almost from the beginning of his association with the *Edinburgh* he had been at the centre of most of its political rows. From his early essays through to the Reform Bill debates and beyond Macaulay had surrounded himself with and indeed seemed almost deliberately to provoke controversy. Most of the Review's extended quarrels in the early thirties were of his making.

His shrewd tactic of reviewing a late edition of Mill's *Essay on Government*, in March 1829, had the desired effect of rekindling the *Westminster*'s animus against the *Edinburgh*, and presenting a challenge which had to be answered. Macaulay's impressive critique of Utilitarian theories of government resulted in a six-part debate, three articles by Macaulay in the *Edinburgh* in 1829, and three responses in the *Westminster*. The contest was not only generally agreed to have been his personal victory, but had the more tangible result of bringing him to the attention of Lord Lansdowne, who offered him the parliamentary seat for Calne in February 1830. Politics and literature in this instance, it might have been said, worked hand in hand.[21]

Not all of Macaulay's self-generated controversies were on such a comparatively high intellectual plane. A passage in his review of Southey's *Colloquies* (January 1830) accused that writer of admiring soldiers and delighting in 'snuffing up carnage', an accusation which made Napier profoundly uneasy and which produced immediate attacks in *Fraser's* and in *Blackwood's*. The offensive comment was omitted when the essay was reprinted.

It was not unusual for quarrels to extend beyond the Review. Macaulay was no novice at pamphlet warfare. His review of Robert Montgomery's *Poems* (April 1830), an attack on the still persistent practice of puffing, arose partly because Montgomery had attacked Macaulay in his satire, *The Age Reviewed* (1827). Macaulay's review was then answered in a note to Montgomery's *Oxford: a Poem* (1831). His review of Robert Sadler's *Law of Population* (July 1830) produced a rejoinder by Sadler, which accused Macaulay of ignorance and deliberate falsification and urged him to remove from his work 'the towering and noxious plant of a conceited and contemptuous self-sufficiency which always grows more luxuriantly upon the meanest soils'. In his 'Sadler's 'Refutation' Refuted' in the January 1831 *Edinburgh* Macaulay declared that Sadler 'foams at the mouth with the love of truth and vindicates the Divine benevolence with a most edifying heartiness of hatred'.[22]

It was scarcely the language of intellectual debate. It was the language of a former reviewing era. *Blackwood's* then took up Sadler's cause with 'Mr. Sadler and the Edinburgh Reviewer. A Prolusion in three Chapters' by John Wilson (February 1831), which undertook to vindicate Sadler 'from one of the basest attacks ever made by ignorance and folly on learning and wisdom'. Macaulay reported that he could not get through it, and that 'it bore the same relation to Sadler's pamphlet that a bad hash bears to a bad joint'.[23] Sadler replied to Macaulay's second article but by this time the combatants had run out of steam. There was a certain stylized element in the quarrel, but just how much both sides regarded the activity as a set piece is difficult to judge. The dispute had a significant tailpiece when Sadler opposed Macaulay in the election for Leeds in 1832. Sadler's reported personal bitterness at his defeat suggested that the *Edinburgh* fracas had been more than just a routine skirmish.

Macaulay was a pugnacious reviewer who delighted in a challenge, loved a good fight, and was unafraid to criticize. He was also, like Croker, inexhaustible in his concentration on detail once he got his teeth into an issue. All of this, accompanied by his prodigious literary skills, made him an outstanding reviewer. It also made him, occasionally, something of a liability.

Two publications related to Sir James Mackintosh, the much revered Whig philosopher and historian, produced a flutter of expectation in reviewing circles, both Whig and Tory, in 1834-5. His fragmentary *History of the Revolution in England in 1688* was published in 1834 and completed by William Wallace, the editor, who also added a biographical sketch of Mackintosh. This was followed in 1835 by the official two volume *Memoirs of the Life of Mackintosh* edited by Mackintosh's son. Macaulay was the obvious reviewer for the *History* and the advance sheets were dispatched to India. He completed the review by December 1834 but delays in the mails meant that the article was not published until July 1835. The writing was complicated by the fact that Wallace's biographical sketch was not initially included in the first set of sheets which were sent to him.

Macaulay's review of the *History*, which coincided with Croker's review of the *Life* in the *Quarterly*, was a spirited defence by a loyal disciple who openly admitted to 'feelings of respect and gratitude which might possibly pervert our judgment'. His real critical fire was reserved for the hapless editor, who, he alleged, had produced a 'calumnious' biographical sketch, and a continuation 'unworthy' of the history. 'Why such an artist was selected to deface so fine a Torso, we cannot pretend to conjecture... He affects and for aught we know, feels something like contempt for the celebrated man whose life he has undertaken to write.' As a historian, Macaulay suggested, the editor, who was not named either in the review or on the title page of the volume, was interested only in the latest and most fashionable ideas. 'What most disgusts us is the contempt with which the writer thinks fit to speak of all things that were done before the coming in of the very latest fashion in politics...' He was 'a man who is a very bad specimen of the English of the nineteeenth century — a man who knows nothing but what it is a scandal not to know' (Vol. LXI, 281, 284).

Strong words, but not beyond the accepted bounds of propriety, and not, it would seem, without foundation. Croker too, in his June 1834 review of the *History* in the *Quarterly*, had commmented on the 'tone of disparagement and censure' which had characterized the biographical sketch, censure that 'ought not to have been hazarded without the exhibition of solid proof'. He also noted that the editor had continued the *History*, 'though not of Sir James's school' (Vol. LI, 493).

Wallace, the editor, clearly thought otherwise, and promptly issued a challenge to the editor of the *Edinburgh Review* and to the unnamed reviewer. Empson and Napier were thrown into a state of panic. Empson took legal advice to the effect that Wallace was precluded from demanding the satisfaction of a gentleman from any such language as was contained in the review. Macaulay, still in India, was puzzled, and quite rightly pointed out that Wallace could not be so absurd as to think that criticism of an anonymous work could justify a demand for personal satisfaction.[24]

The ability of an anonymous author to challenge an anonymous reviewer had already been tested in an exchange between Albany Fonblanque and Brougham in 1830, when the former demanded satisfaction for the latter's comments in the *Edinburgh* on an anonymous article he had written in the *Westminster*. Lord Dudley in this instance had given his judgement which hung on the circumstances of anonymity and 'the nonsense', as Brougham's most recent biographer termed it, was soon forgotten.[25]

Nonsense it might have been in this case as well, but Wallace was not so easily dissuaded. He clearly relished this sort of activity. According to John Allen he fought a bloodless duel with

Mackintosh's son shortly after the publication of the *Life*. He dropped the challenge to Napier, but Empson and others feared he might renew the challenge to Macaulay on his return from India. In preparation for this Empson proposed various strategies, including making Macaulay promise not to take any step without consulting him, on pain of taking both Wallace and him to Bow Street to swear to keep the peace. In the end the matter was resolved by a diplomatic formula, to the immense relief of Empson and the more philosophical satisfaction of Macaulay. Wallace formally agreed that he had meant nothing disrespectful or unkind to Mackintosh in his 'Memoir' and Macaulay expressed his regret that his language with regard to Wallace had seemed personally offensive.[26]

Duelling over an anonymous review seemed an anachronism in 1838, as indeed it was, a harking back to the early days of *Blackwood's*, the Scott–Christie affair, and the atmosphere of squibs, lampoons and crude political satire which had characterized the period from 1817 onward. The savagery of the political satire, manifested not only by *Blackwood's*, but by a host of minor papers, had rubbed off, to a certain extent, on the more sober elements of the periodical press during the period.

Robust and pugnacious the quarterlies may have been, but the scurrility and personal savagery of *Blackwood's* was something which they found regrettable, as Jeffrey's response to Scott about party politics demonstrated. The general dismay with which Lockhart's appointment to the *Quarterly* was greeted, a dismay based mainly on his *Blackwood* past, suggested that in 1825 the *Quarterly* too was anxious to dissociate itself once and for all from that era and to put on a more statesmanlike public mien. Scott was keen to press the point upon Lockhart when he counselled him prior to signing the *Quarterly* contract that 'personal violence and abuse is now stale and tiresome... I have a notion people are disgusted with it and that a controversialist had better shoot balls than pelt with rotten eggs'.[27]

The rivalry between the *Edinburgh* and the *Quarterly* had altered perceptibly in character since the early days. The raucous and splenetic atmosphere in which, as Jeffrey had admitted, there was too great a play on personality had almost disappeared. Traces remained, as in the Macaulay–Sadler dispute, but the general atmosphere was more sedate and the quarrels gentlemanly. Croker represented an interesting throwback, his reviewing often treading a thin line between what was just about acceptable and what was not. He tailored his style somewhat to accommodate the new mood after

1831, but it still retained an anachronistic acerbity, a feeling of suppressed rage, and the sense of a thin layer of decorum always about to be breached. 'Violence nowadays does not answer so well as it did 30 years ago,' Lockhart had felt obliged to warn him as late as 1849. He could have done with the warning much earlier on.[30]

Croker apart, the relationship between the two quarterlies now resembled that between two long-established rival firms, respectful of the fact that they had been in the same business for a long time. Editors and contributors alike, however, still kept a weather eye on the competition. Both camps buzzed with gossip, the authorship of significant articles, gleeful tittle tattle about mishaps and blunders, and rumours as to when the other side would respond to a challenge. Lockhart's determination to bring the *Quarterly* out ahead of the *Edinburgh*, on the assumption that most people read both and that it was sensible to steal a march on the competition, was a shrewd move, even though it did not always work out in practice.

News travelled quickly. Allen reported the details of Lord Mahon's war with the *Quarterly* to Napier very shortly after the offending article appeared in April 1833, including the news that Mahon intended to reprint the original article to demonstrate the extent of Croker's alterations (see above p. 65). When the *Quarterly* made another blunder in 1835, probably in one of its political articles, Croker commented wearily to Lockhart, 'How these things must please Mr. Macvey Napier and Lord B & V'.[29]

Reviewers for politically sensitive subjects were chosen with care. Given Sir James Mackintosh's prominence in Whig circles prior to 1830 his *History* and the *Life* were obvious occasions for political point scoring. Napier was willing to accept the delay which would result from Macaulay's undertaking the *History* and persuaded Jeffrey to do the *Life*. Croker no doubt accepted both tasks in the knowledge that Macaulay would be his opposite number in at least one. His review of the *Life* was a surprisingly sympathetic and generous assessment of a political contemporary for whom he clearly felt considerable sympathy, and who, he argued, had been shabbily treated by the younger generation of Whigs after 1830. His review of the *History* in June 1834, pointedly entitled 'Revolutions of 1688 and 1831', was more of a party political piece, designed to awaken the public to what he saw as the dangers inherent in Reform. Both sides claimed to have been wounded in the exchanges. Lockhart reported that they had been taken to task in the *Edinburgh* while Allen hoped that Napier would have an antidote to the *Quarterly*'s 'poison', an unusually prickly response from an otherwise phlegmatic reviewer. In fact both sides handled their reviews with admirable restraint. The only near victim was Macaulay at the hands of the enraged Wallace.

The Duke of Wellington's *Despatches* was another potentially sensitive subject. Napier and Empson took enormous pains to canvass various contacts for a reviewer who could deal adequately with the book. Sir William Napier, the military historian, refused, having agreed to do it for the *Westminster*, and pointed out that his views of the way the Duke had been treated by the Whigs would prove unacceptable. Another reviewer declined because he had been too close to the Duke. G. R. Gleig, the historian and novelist, was also floated, and finally Sir George Murray, a confidential friend of the Duke's, according to John Allen, and a one time *Quarterly* reviewer, emerged. He was given a free hand as to time and length, and extra-tight precautions were taken to protect his anonymity. After such a trawling, the review appears to have gone virtually unremarked, except for Henry Rich's comment that he wished a less Tory reviewer could have been found, and Allen's report that the Duke was pleased with the review. Croker had reviewed the work in the *Quarterly* eighteen months earlier, with no repercussions.[30]

Considering the extensive deliberations over James Stephen's suitability to review the *Life of Wilberforce* (April 1838, see above p. 32), the furore caused by Brougham's taking up of the Clarkson cause must have earmarked the subject as one fraught with troubles all round. Croker reviewed the *Life* in the *Quarterly* but deliberately chose not to enter the new dispute, seeing it very much as a domestic issue. Croker's fire in 1837 had been reserved for a nicely aggressive attack on Lord John Russell (October 1837) which Lockhart regarded as a model piece, and which Henry Rich described as a 'tissue of evasions, quibbles and falsehoods'. Rich begged the right of reply and did so in the April 1838 *Edinburgh*, with Russell's help and support. Croker's energies in 1838 were concentrated on Lister's *Life of Lord Clarendon* (October 1838). Lister had been lobbying Napier to have the work reviewed in the *Edinburgh* by Macaulay, and if not, by Allen or Empson. Empson reviewed it in the end (January 1839) but Allen used Lister's pamphlet published in reply to Croker in a further article, 'Charles the First and the Scottish Commissioners' the following April.[31]

All of this suggests that the Reviews watched one another warily, but that the days of out and out war had come to an end. A certain amount of fraternizing took place beween the two camps, particularly among the older generation. Scott had relished the fact, and had also been touched, as he told George Ellis, that in all their discussions about party politics in the *Edinburgh*, Jeffrey had no inkling that his old friend was intent on founding a rival quarterly. Their personal regard for one another, though shaken by that event, remained until the end, and Scott's journal from 1826 onward recorded several congenial dinners at Jeffrey's home, prior to the latter's departure for the Lord Advocate's office. On one occasion he reflected:

> I do not know why it is that when I am with a party of my Opposition friends, the day is often the merrier than with our own set. Is it because they are cleverer? Jeffrey and Henry Cockburn are, to be sure, very extraordinary men, yet it is not owing to that entirely. I believe both parties meet with the feeling of something like novelty. We have not worn out our jests in daily contact. There is also a disposition on such occasions to be courteous and of course to be pleased.[32]

Jeffrey found no difficulty in consorting with his old rivals once in London, and confided freely to Lockhart and others about Napier's trials with Brougham. Lockhart reported to Croker:

> As for Brougham, Jeffrey told us on Saturday 'half this business wd. send you or me or any other man to the bottomless pit — but w. him tis only B's *way* — he is known to be cracky & that covers all'.[33]

The incorrigible Brougham, once his influence with the *Edinburgh* gave every sign of being on the wane, promptly courted the opposition, much to their surprise and embarrassment. Persistence paid off. Between 1845 and 1854, he contributed to the *Quarterly* on an irregular basis, sometimes on political subjects, but more usually on the safer grounds of history and literature. One of the more unlikely and yet touching developments in the history of the two quarterlies was the growing friendship between Brougham and Croker in their later years. After nearly half a century of rivalry in the Reviews and in the House of Commons Empson reported to Napier in the autumnn of 1838 that Brougham could be seen walking about Dover arm in arm with Croker. Brougham's final years were marked by a softening of the old acerbity, a decrease in his aggressiveness, and a return to what his journal called his 'antient friends', including Jeffrey.

The younger generation on the whole seemed both less gregarious socially and more conscious of the traditional rivalries. Napier's retiring nature and general diffidence reinforced by his reluctance to leave Edinburgh for more than a few weeks in the spring made him a shadowy figure to all but his closest associates. Lockhart's reserve similarly made him an unlikely focus for any *Quarterly* salon. Murray maintained the traditional hospitality of Albemarle Street. Lockhart participated in some of this, but to most people he remained a remote and somewhat unattractive figure.

Disraeli's now famous jibe, made with reference to Lockhart's enthusiastic review of James Morier's novel, *Zohrab the Hostage* in the *Quarterly* (December 1832), that he would like to review it himself in order 'to show the public the consequence of having a tenth rate novelist at the head of a great critical journal', acquires an added dimension with knowledge of their earlier association. The comment no doubt pleased Napier, as it was intended to do. As a result of the *Representative* débâcle Disraeli was *persona non grata* with the *Quarterly* and he was anxious to establish a reviewing base in 'your classic journal', as he later told Napier.[34] Political commitments intervened to prevent this, but the remark lingered in reviewing circles as an example of the waspish mood of the times. It was pure malice on Disraeli's part, and the 'tenth rate' taunt was nicely aimed at the author of *Valerius*, *Adam Blair* and *Reginald Dalton* from a colleague who, if not yet a first rate novelist, was on his way.

But considering the number of highly talented, sensitive, not to say egocentric contributors involved in both Reviews over a decade, there were remarkably few personal clashes of any moment in the 1830s. Brougham and Macaulay, though never reconciled, went their separate ways after 1840, with mutual relief. Brougham and Napier, too, parted exhausted, and later effected a muted reconciliation. There was one clash of personalities, however, which more than compensated for the dearth. The antagonism of Croker and Macaulay, which began in the House of Commons and then spilled over into their reviewing, was to have reverberations in both publications for nearly fifty years.

Whatever his deficiencies, after his return in 1831, Croker was the *Quarterly*'s most eminent reviewer, the counterpart of Macaulay in the *Edinburgh*. The two first found themselves in opposition in the

Reform Bill debates in the spring of 1831. It was in some ways a curious match. There was a difference of twenty years in their ages, which effectively meant a difference of a generation. Croker was a Tory elder statesman, an experienced parliamentarian and a practised reviewer with two decades of reviewing behind him. Like Macaulay he possessed a wide range of intellectual interests apart from politics, particularly history, biography and literature. Macaulay's political fortunes were in the ascendancy. Croker's were about to enter upon their decline.

Macaulay's parliamentary reputation was made during this period. He began to speak during the second reading of the Reform Bill, only months after his re-election for Calne in August 1830. His speeches, carefully prepared, eloquent, powerful and delivered with effortless flow, increased his already impressive standing within his party and beyond. Croker, like Brougham, viewed the precocious upstart with increasing irritation. Croker, too, was an able speaker, his strength lying in quick rebuttal and retort, and an enviable command of facts, skills which were the antithesis of Macaulay's. During the debates, Croker was sometimes on his feet as many as five times in one night to challenge Macaulay.

It was a case of instant antipathy. Croker later admitted to Lockhart that he had disliked Macaulay the moment he saw him, even before he heard him speak. It was an antipathy, however, in which each recognized that he had met his match.[35] The parliamentary antagonism assumed an added dimension in the summer of 1831 with the publication of Croker's long awaited edition of Boswell's *Life of Johnson*. Macaulay was determined to review it for the *Edinburgh*. 'An impudent, leering Croker' had made some sarcastic remarks at his expense in the House, Macaulay wrote to his sister; 'See whether I do not dust that varlet's jacket for him in the next number of the Blue and Yellow. I detest him more than cold boiled veal.'[36]

The review, when it appeared in September, was crotchety and tiresomely detailed. 'This work has greatly disappointed us,' it began. It was 'ill-compiled, ill arranged, ill expressed and ill printed'. 'Nothing in the work has astonished us so much as the ignorance or carelessness of Mr. Croker with respect to facts and dates.' (Vol. LIV, 1) This was followed by a remorseless list of the disputed details, one of Macaulay's standard reviewing tactics, as wearying to the modern as, one assumes, to the contemporary reader, after which the review moved into a general essay on Johnson in his best 'essay-like review' manner.

The review, in the number for September 1831, was actually published on 8 October, just after some particularly fraught exchanges with Croker in the House. 'I have, though I say it who should not say it, beaten Croker black and blue. Impudent as he is, I think he must be ashamed of the pickle in which I leave him,' Macaulay wrote triumphantly to his sister.[37]

The *Westminster* entered the fray the same month, praising the accuracy of one of Croker's anecdotes which Macaulay had claimed was erroneous. Macaulay was delighted: 'John Mill is in a foaming rage, and says they are in a worse scrape than Croker: — John Murray says that it is a damned nuisance: and Croker looks across the House of Commons at me with a leer of hatred which I repay with a gracious smile of pity,' he wrote to Ellis. But most of Macaulay's alleged errors proved not to be so. Croker supplied Lockhart with a series of proofs of the erroneousness of Macaulay's 'corrections', which were published in *Blackwood's* and then produced as a pamphlet, 'Answers to the Edinburgh Reviewer of Croker's Boswell selected from *Blackwood's Magazine*' (1831). Macaulay professed to be able to 'blow it to atoms in a note', but then decided against it: 'I thought that a contest with your grog-drinking, cock-fighting, cudgel-playing Professor of Moral Philosophy [John Wilson] would be too degrading,' he told Napier.[38]

But in fact the *Blackwood's* article successfully answered a number of the charges of inaccuracy, and reduced others to insignificance. The substance of this article was reprinted in later editions of the Boswell in order to lay the ghost of the charge of inaccuracy once and for all. Macaulay's review had created the desired sensation, but the ultimate victory was Croker's. His edition remained a standard one until the twentieth century.

The Croker–Macaulay dispute, however, had only just begun. It was of course only one element in the now ritualized rivalry between the two Reviews, but its sharply personalized nature made it unique. In some respects it was not unlike the near libellous assaults of the old days, and the ferocity of feeling struck an uncomfortable as well as an anachronistic note in the 1830s and 1840s and beyond, a note which jarred awkwardly with the current reviewing temper.

The quarrel was exacerbated by the publication of certain key works. Lockhart's long awaited *Life of Scott* was tactfully omitted from notice by the *Quarterly*, but less explicably it was not reviewed by the *Edinburgh* either. Herman Merivale had offered, as had Bulwer Lytton, but Napier and Empson were agreed that the biography should be reserved for Macaulay. To Napier's discomfiture, Macaulay refused, insisting that he had never felt competent to review works of literature but, more significantly, saying that he felt a strong disapproval of aspects of Scott's life and personality, notably his political partisanship and his unbecoming eagerness for money — opinions, he reasonably argued, which would be highly unpopular in a Scottish review, even if a Whig one. There were negative murmurings from other potential reviewers as well. Both Sir David Brewster and John Allen thought Lockhart had not been sufficiently in sympathy with his subject but neither was willing to commit himself in print. More by default than by design the *Life* went unnoticed, which could not but have been taken as a slight to the *Quarterly*. Macaulay's *Lays of Ancient Rome*, on the other hand, was reviewed sympathetically by Henry Hart Milman (March 1843) and the revised edition of Lockhart's translation of *Ancient Spanish Ballads* received a commendation in the January 1841 *Edinburgh*.

As reviewers, Croker and Macaulay were attracted to the same kinds of non-political works, particularly history and biography, a point which they and their editors noted carefully. It was not surprising that Croker should have been the *Quarterly*'s reviewer of Mackintosh's *History* as well as of the *Life* and that Macaulay would almost certainly review at least one of them in the *Edinburgh*. What Croker did not relish was to be thought to be copying Macaulay. He deliberately put off an article on Mirabeau which he could have done with ease and enjoyment in 1835 because of Macaulay's article in the July 1832 *Edinburgh*. He similarly rejected an article on Walpole because of Macaulay's October 1833 review of Walpole's *Letters* and after Lockhart invited him to consider whether 'it wd. not be *infra dig* and doing Tom too much honour'. [39]

The next public encounter arose precisely because of this collision of interests. As we have seen, Croker's bad tempered and ungenerous review of Fanny Burney's memoirs of her father in April 1833 had turned into an ungentlemanly attack on her reputation. Croker had had the parish registers of Lynn, in Norfolk, searched in order to prove that she had not been, as was generally thought, a young girl of seventeen when she wrote her first novel, *Evelina*, but rather a mature woman of twenty-five. Literary rather than personal vanity had permitted this deception, Croker argued, but the fact of her age significantly altered the general attitude to the novel.

The 'discovery' of her age was repeated, nearly nine years later, in his subsequent review of Madame d'Arblay's *Diary and Letters* (June

1842). The second article presented an extremely unsympathetic portrait of Miss Burney when Keeper of the Robes to Queen Charlotte, using Croker's favourite practice of copious but well-chosen extracts designed to permit the subject to condemn herself. His main attack was directed towards what he saw as Fanny Burney's egocentricity, her self-pity, her determination to turn everything into a reflection on herself and to present an unflattering portrait of the Royal Household.

Incensed by the tenor of Croker's article as well as by its imputations, the Burney family offered Macaulay 'papers and communications' if he would 'fight their battle against Croker'. Macaulay somewhat reluctantly agreed to review the *Diary and Letters* in the January 1843 *Edinburgh*. His review presented an interesting contrast both in technique and in substance. It was a sympathetic picture of an intelligent woman, forced through her father's ambition and her own vanity into a role which turned her into a slave and a pauper. It concluded with an assessment of her strengths and weaknesses as a novelist, another 'essay-like review' in Macaulay's characteristic manner, and, as with the essay on Johnson, totally undercutting his own point that he was not qualified to write literary criticism. Macaulay (Vol. LXXVI, 537) alluded to the widely accepted belief that *Evelina* had been written when she was seventeen, adding, 'Frances was too honest to confirm it. Probably she was too much of a woman to contradict it', and concluding that she had had many other critics, but it had never occurred to them:

> to search the parish register of Lynn in order that they might be able to twit a lady with having concealed her age. That exploit was reserved for a writer of our own time, whose spite she provoked by not furnishing him with materials for a worthless edition of Boswell's *Life of Johnson*, some sheets of which our readers have doubtless seen round parcels of better books.

Macaulay originally added, 'We wonder a little at the severity with which we have heard him censured on this account. In any other man's life this would, we own, have been a serious stain. In his, it is hardly a speck.' Had he been writing under his own name, Macaulay told Napier, he would have added still more: 'It is merely a speck in the life of one who got a good place by playing the spy on a courtesan in his youth, and a good legacy by turning parasite to a whole seraglio of courtesans in his old age,' a sentence which was undoubtedly libellous. It was, he claimed, only the fear that Croker, like Wallace, might show fight and issue a challenge to Napier, which caused him to reject the addition. Napier was so agitated by the first proposed addition that Macaulay did not press the second, and at Napier's insistence, neither appeared in the final review, which packed a sufficient punch as it stood.[40]

The episode offers an interesting insight into Macaulay, a man who although pugnacious, did not usually hold grudges, and who regarded the cut and thrust of reviewing as a normal part of a day's work. Croker had clearly got under his skin. His dislike of him was deeper than his feelings for any of his other opponents, apart, possibly from Brougham, and it did not diminish with time.

With that one albeit foreshortened paragraph, the embers of the old quarrel, begun over ten years earlier in the House of Commons and carried into the review of the Boswell, were fanned into flame. Lockhart was irritated that Milman's generally favourable review of the *Lays* was on the stocks, but not yet published. To be seen to come forward two months later in magnanimous praise of Macaulay was almost more than he could bear. The pointed omission of a review of Macaulay's *Essays* was undoubtedly in retaliation for the Burney challenge.

But Macaulay's reputation was effortlessly rising. There was little his old opponents could do that would not seem deliberately churlish or dog-in-the-mangerish. The peak was reached with the publication of the first two volumes of the *History* in 1849. Lockhart this time agreed that it would be 'wrong & silly' to pass over it in silence. Croker was by no means determined to review it, nor did Lockhart encourage him, no doubt fearing that if he attempted to demolish it the *Quarterly* would inevitably place itself in a critical wilderness and appear ridiculous. When Croker did decide to do the review, Lockhart was pleased but cautious:

> I have only to say that I don't know who else cd. review that book in a manner suitable for the Q.R. ... but that I have been afraid of your very natural feeling of personal dislike to the man. Now I do not think such feeling shd. animate the Q.R. — ... I know that he has been unjust & insolent to you — but still he is one of the most vigorous writers of his time & I think any disparagement of his intellectual powers wd. tell only against the review.

Both Lockhart and Murray took a hand in the review, outlining what they thought should be Croker's main lines of argument, cautioning him against lengthy catalogues of errors, reminding him to emphasize the famous third chapter, urging him to stress Macaulay's antipathy to the clergy, and by what Murray called 'the old sun and wind rule', to find something to praise, such as his treatment of the death of Charles II and the reign of James II.

All in all, they kept a fairly tight rein, and Croker agreed to most of their suggestions. The review was sent to Lockhart in slips from the printers. He in turn consulted Murray and relayed his responses back to Croker. They consulted experts on specific points, and both constantly urged Croker to moderate the tone. Lockhart affected an apology for the latter request:

> Neither he [Murray] nor I ever participated in the heat of parliamentary conflict & you must make allowance for our not quite entering into their vehemence.[41]

The review, when it appeared in the March 1849 number, was eighty-two pages in length, ungenerous and petty. It contained a catalogue of allegedly erroneous details, referred to the paucity and irregularity of Macaulay's dates, claimed that he was unreliable in his use of sources, and then focused on the larger charge of unacknowledged reliance on Mackintosh's *History of the Revolution in England in 1688*. Macaulay made the facts of history as fabulous as his Lays did those of the Roman tradition, Croker suggested. The history was written in bad taste, bad feeling and bad faith. (Both Macaulay and Croker enjoyed these balanced catalogues of insults.)

The nub of Croker's attack was that Macaulay was writing both Whig history and 'imaginative' history. He was 'a great painter but a suspicious narrator, a grand proficient in the picturesque, but a very poor professor of the historic.' He concluded that the work 'will be devoured with the same eagerness that Oliver Twist and Vanity Fair excite, but the work will hardly find a place on the historic shelf' (Vol. LXXXIV, 630).

Not surprisingly Croker's review had an encouraging effect on the *Quarterly*'s sales, and also sparked off a controversy in *The Times* and other papers. But it was virtually a lone voice in the rhapsodic chorus of praise which greeted the *History* and crowned Macaulay's reputation. Macaulay was nonplussed and noted in his diary:

> His blunders are really incredible. The article has been received with general contempt. Really Croker has done me a great service: ... He should have been large in acknowledgement; should have taken a mild

and expostulatory tone; and should have looked for real blemishes, which, as I too well know, he might easily have found. Instead of that he has written with such rancour as to make everybody sick. I could almost pity him. But he is a bad, a very bad man: a scandal to politics and to letters.[42]

And there the matter rested, until 1876. Just as in 1837 the publication of Lockhart's *Life of Scott* had rubbed an old sore of Jeffrey's, so in 1876, the publication of G. O. Trevelyan's *Life and Letters of Lord Macaulay* breathed new life into the old quarrel even though the antagonists were both dead. Writing of Macaulay's pugnacity, Trevelyan quoted from the letter to Napier in January 1843 detailing the unsavoury portions of Croker's private life and the scandals of his literary life, adding that Macaulay's comments clearly indicated that his animosity to Croker arose from incompatibility of moral sentiments and not merely of political opinions. Later, he added the following comment:

> Macaulay's judgment has been confirmed by the public voice which rightly or wrongly identifies Croker with the character of Rigby in Mr. Disraeli's *Coningsby*.[43]

More provocatively still, in the second volume Trevelyan published the passage from Macaulay's diary for April 1849 in which he recorded his reaction to Croker's review of the *History*.

With the appearance of the last sentence, 'But he is a bad, a very bad man: a scandal to politics and to letters', it was as though the 1830s had suddenly returned. Henry Reeve, the editor of the *Edinburgh*, reviewed Trevelyan himself (April 1876). It was the expected tribute to the Review's most distinguished contributor in later years, beginning by alluding to two men born in the early years of the century, who were 'destined to exercise no common influence over the literature of their country and the opinions of their own ages, and possibly of all future time'. Not Macaulay and Croker but Macaulay and Mill. Writing about the reception of the *History*, Reeve noted that in 'one instance alone was a serious attempt made to depreciate the merit and detract from the influence of one of the greatest historical works of our time', adding comfortably, 'as was said at the time, the writer of the article, in attempting murder, had committed suicide'. And then came the astonishingly bitter accusation which disturbed the urbane surface of the review (Vol. CXLIII, 572–3):

From that day to this, the same Journal has never lost an opportunity of launching shafts against the literary reputation of Lord Macaulay. Mr. Croker is dead, but the race of Crokers is not extinct, nor is it likely to expire as long as the principal organ of the Tory party keeps it sedulously alive.

This was published in April 1876. In July the *Quarterly* returned with two articles, a review of Trevelyan by Gladstone and an article on Croker by William Smith, the *Quarterly*'s editor. The latter was ostensibly a review of a new edition of Croker's Boswell and a 30-year-old collection of his essays on the French Revolution, but its real purpose was an attempt to rehabilitate Croker, or at least to bolster his reputation in the face of Trevelyan or, as Smith put it, 'to redeem his memory from being handed down as a mere victim of Macaulay's affected contempt and unaffected ire'. Smith came close to admitting that Croker sometimes overstepped the mark in his reviewing:

> his sarcastic sallies and pungent wit made him many enemies, nor can it be denied that he frequently indulged in personal allusions, the like of which we had hoped previous to the appearance of Mr. Trevelyan's book, had now disappeared from literature.

His early manhood, Smith offered by way of explanation, was passed in a time of bitter personal animosity, 'when there was hardly any social intercourse between persons of different political opinions and party spirit proceeded to lengths unknown to the present generation. He was himself aware that he was frequently betrayed into too great severity towards literary and political opponents' (Vol. CXLII, 107).

Gladstone's review of Trevelyan was generous in its tribute to Macaulay's place in literature and politics, but he singled out by way of criticism 'a more than ordinary defect in the mental faculty of appreciating opponents. He did not fully take the measure of those from whom he differed in the things wherein he differed.' He instanced (Vol. CXLII, 22–3) three of Macaulay's personal antipathies to whom his behaviour was less than generous — Peel, Brougham and Croker, adding in the case of the last:

> It is yet more to be lamented that ... he carried the passion of politics into the Elysian fields of literature, and that the scales in which he tried the merits of Croker's edition of Boswell seem to have been weighted, on the descending side, with his recollections of parliamentary collision.

Both Smith and Gladstone were correct in spotting the weakness of their subjects. Croker and Macaulay allowed personal antipathy to prevail over critical judgement, to the detriment of their own reputations and temporarily those of the journals for which they wrote.

It was not so much a case of the traditional political rivalry of the *Edinburgh* and the *Quarterly* being fought out in the Elysian fields of literature as of literary journals providing an arena for a fierce personal antagonism that had its origin in political opposition. The ferocity of personal feelings in this instance made the dispute unique, unique at least in the context of the 1830s and 1840s. 'Violence nowadays does not answer so well as it did 30 years ago,' as Lockhart had warned Croker before he began the review of the *History*. By violence essentially he meant the play of personality. And he was, generally speaking, right. But he underestimated the strength of feeling on both sides.

As a case study the Macaulay–Croker affair is interesting in the way in which the fragile edifice of anonymity and the corporate voice proved totally unable to withstand the force of powerful personalities. The star system was at its most obvious and anonymity seemed, at least in retrospect, a mere charade.

The affair is interesting too for the longevity of the dispute, the way in which it became part of the living history of the two Reviews. The fact that the quarterlies spanned several generations meant that they could respond to their own history as it was being written. Jeffrey had done so in 1844. The editors at mid-century similarly experienced the scrutiny of critics like Bagehot and Stephen and later Morley, when the appearance of collected essays and the memoirs of early reviewers provided an opportunity. Forty-five years after the Reform Bill debates and the appearance of Croker's *Boswell*, several paragraphs of Trevelyan's *Life* were able to trigger off the old antagonism.

The Croker–Macaulay affair was not really a political argument. It was too closely bound up with personality to be ideological. But to the next generation it summarized the old rivalry, the traditional opposition, and that opposition was at least in part a political one. The *Edinburgh* defended Macaulay warts and all, but acknowledged the warts. The *Quarterly* did the same for Croker. In the moribund seventies it must have seemed, at least for the moment, an exhilarating return to more lively times.

Henry Reeve, who presided over the *Edinburgh* longer than any other nineteenth-century editor, from July 1855 to October 1895, described his translation from a leader writer on *The Times* to the editorship of the *Edinburgh* as 'a sort of peerage as compared with the tumult of the Lower House'.[44] He could not have made the analogy twenty years earlier, in the 1830s, when the respective roles of the quarterlies and the newspapers were so different.

But the thirties were probably the last period when the worlds of politics and literature combined in a meaningful way within the context of quarterly reviews. Ministerial journalism, as Stephen Koss has noted, effectively entered its terminal phase with Brougham.[45] The days of real political influence were over by the early 1840s, if not before. As the power of the newspaper press grew, the political role of the quarterlies declined, and their political decline, as Jeffrey had seen as early as 1808, ultimately spelled their general demise.

Notes

1. Francis Jeffrey, *Contributions to the Edinburgh Review*, 4 vols (London: Longman, 1844), I, xiv–xv.
2. Scott, *Letters*, II, 105.
3. Scott, *Letters*, II, 138.
4. Jeffrey, *Contributions*, I, xiv–xv; *Napier*, pp.434–5.
5. Scott, *Letters*, II, 142; *Croker Papers*, II, 229–30; partially reprinted in Brightfield, pp.407–8.
6. *Croker Papers*, I, 26.
7. Carlyle, *Letters*,V, 311.
8. BL Add. MSS. 34617, f.577.
9. BL Add. MSS. 34615, ff.37, 462.
10. BL Add. MSS. 34615, ff.413, 337, 406, 300; 34617, f.139.
11. BL Add. MSS. 34616, f.89; 34618, ff.403, 581.
12. BL Add. MSS. 34615, f.87; 34618, f.130.
13. Scott, *Journal*, I, 307; II, 181.
14. Scott, *Letters*, X, 421.
15. Smiles, *Memoir of John Murray*, II, 52.
16. BL Add. MSS. 34615, ff.55, 37, 126.
17. Lockhart to Croker, 4 April 1835, 12 March 1836, 2 September 1836, quoted by Lott, pp.164, 177, 183; Lockhart–Croker Correspondence, *Notes and Queries*, 21 October 1944.
18. BL Add. MSS. 34618, f.434.
19. BL Add. MSS. 34618, f. 231.
20. Macaulay, *Letters*, III, 195.

21. For a discussion of the Mill–Macaulay debate, see Jack Lively and John Rees, ed, *Utilitarian Logic and Politics: James Mill's 'Essay on Government', Macaulay's Critique and the Ensuing Debate* (Oxford: Clarendon Press, 1978).

22. Robert Sadler, *A Refutation of an Article in the Edinburgh Review* (1831); see Macaulay, *Letters*, I, 262 n4, 318 n8, 268n.

23. Macaulay, *Letters*, I, 318–9, 318n8.

24. BL Add. MSS. 34616, f.119; Macaulay, *Letters*, III, 171.

25. Robert Stewart, *Henry Brougham 1778–1868: His Public Career* (London: Bodley Head, 1985), p.207 n2.

26. BL Add. MSS. 34619, ff.143, 42; Macaulay, *Letters*, III, 244, 253–4.

27. Scott, *Letters*, IX, 251.

28. Lockhart–Croker Correspondence, *Notes and Queries*, 20 April 1946.

29. BL Add. MSS. 34616, f.79; Croker to Lockhart [nd. 1835], Murray Papers.

30. BL Add. MSS. 34618 ff.492, 518, 489, 337.

31. BL Add. MSS. 34618, ff.382, 436; 34619, f.54; *Napier*, p.285.

32. Scott, *Journal*, I, 320; *Letters*, II, 138.

33. Lockhart to Croker [1835], in Lott, p.151.

34. Disraeli, *Letters*, I, 239; See also I, 224. Disraeli's taunt was prompted by a supposed insult in Lockhart's review.

35. John Clive, in *Thomas Babington Macaulay: The Shaping of the Historian* (London: Secker and Warburg, 1973), p.193, suggests that the common intellectual interests together with an equivalent social background were a factor in the antipathy. Clive also gives a compelling description of the impact of Macaulay's speeches at this time, pp.157–65.

36. Macaulay, *Letters*, II, 84.

37. Trevelyan, I, 245.

38. Macaulay, *Letters*, II, 106 n4, 110–1.

39. Lockhart to Croker, nd. in Lott, p.137.

40. Macaulay, *Letters*, IV, 63, 89–90, 90 n7.

41. Lockhart–Croker Correspondence, *Notes and Queries*, 20 April, 4 May 1946.

42. Trevelyan, II, 259.

43. Trevelyan, I, 124.

44. J. K. Laughton, *Memoirs of the Life and Correspondence of Henry Reeve* (London: Longman, 1898), I, 339.

45. Stephen Koss, *The Rise and Fall of the Political Press in Britain*, Vol.I (London: Hamish Hamilton, 1981), 46.

Chapter 7

EPILOGUE

In the process of putting the flesh of context on the dry bones of periodical scholarship, to return to John Clive's analogy, the problem has been not only where to begin, but where to stop. I have chosen to discuss the complex web of relationships – personal, ideological, professional and political — which affected the interaction of the *Edinburgh* and the *Quarterly* from the mid-1820s to the early 1840s, all too aware that they were not the only periodicals on the scene. They were, it would be acknowledged, the most significant of the serious critical organs at least until the mid-1830s, but from the 1820s they were gradually surrounded by a growing band of competitors, monthly and weekly rivals as well as other quarterlies.

The foundation of the *Westminster* in 1824 signalled the end of their monopoly, although it took that quarterly over a decade to establish itself as the third member of the great triumvirate of Reviews. In 1827 R. P. Gillies, with Scott's encouragement, launched the *Foreign Quarterly Review* on its precarious course, which was to result, ultimately, in union with the *Westminster* in 1846. Other quarterlies with an interest in foreign literature appeared at the same time, including the *Foreign Review* (1828) and the *British and Foreign Review* (1835) in which Brougham had a hand for a brief time. Other new Reviews, like the High Church *British Critic* (1827) and the *London Review* (1835) edited by J. S. Mill, served specific interest groups, as did a trickle of more specialized quarterlies, including the *Law Magazine* (1828) and the *Quarterly Journal of Education*, published by the Society for the Diffusion of Useful Knowledge.

Apart from the quarterlies, there were a number of serious weekly and monthly Reviews, which made a mark in the 1820s and 1830s, including the Unitarian *Monthly Repository*, founded in 1806 and restyled in 1827, the *Athenaeum* and the *Spectator* (1828), and *Tait's Edinburgh Magazine* (1832). There were the major magazines, *Blackwood's* (1817) and *Fraser's* (1830) and older established monthlies including the *New Monthly* (1814) and the *London Magazine* (1820). There were also older weeklies like the *Examiner* (1808) and William Jerdan's *Literary Gazette* (1817).

All of this puts into perspective Carlyle's moan about the prevalence of reviewing and Hazlitt's more enthusiastic acknowledgement that Reviews and magazines had become a permanent feature of literary life. But despite the proliferation in the 1820s and beyond, Bagehot's assertion that the *Edinburgh* had begun the system and remained the model of reviewing held true until the 1840s.

Ironically, just when it was becoming clear that the great days of the quarterlies' political influence were over, a host of sectarian imitators began to appear: the *Christian Teacher*, later the *Prospective Review* (1835), the *Dublin Review* (1836), the *Church of England Quarterly* (1837), the *North British* (1844), the *British Quarterly* (1845). Few of these had overtly political aims, but sought rather to emulate the general éclat and status of the *Edinburgh* and the *Quarterly*. To have one's own quarterly review had become a mark of intellectual respectability. 'How many Reviews are we to have? Is it not odd that the old ones keep afloat at all?' Lockhart commented to John Wilson in 1844. And Abraham Hayward ventured that 'no new Review, (quarterly at least), will ever succeed. The tendency of the time is against quarterlies.'[1]

Flying in the face of the evidence, quarterly Reviews continued to be founded in the 1850s and into the 1860s, almost as if unaware of the shift of public attention towards monthlies like the *Fortnightly* (1865), the *Contemporary* (1866), the *Nineteenth Century* (1877) and influential weeklies like the *Saturday Review* (1856), the *Spectator* and *The Economist* (1843). The mid-century quarterlies made their mark by the solidity, in the best sense, of their literary criticism, in which they eclipsed their elders. Their tables of contents reflected fiction, poetry, drama, the fine arts, as well as the staples of travel literature, biography and history.

But solid they were, in the best but also the worst sense of the term. The public mood had shifted since the 1830s. The term 'monthly' or 'magazine' no longer suggested frivolity or scurrilousness. Just as the *Edinburgh*'s review format, as Bagehot had observed, had met the need of the time, so the new, shorter articles of the monthlies and weeklies responded to the inclinations of the modern reader. At the end of his editorship, Napier's letters were full of anxiety that the Review was too 'heavy' and that it did not contain enough 'fun'. Bonamy Price, himself an Edinburgh reviewer, pronounced it 'fit for dowagers' in the 1850s.[2] The dangers of dullness, brought on in part by length, which both Napier and Croker had spotted so early on, were now brought home, and with a vengeance.

Bagehot's remark about the appearance of the *Edinburgh* having been regarded as a grave constitutional event, and its composition rumoured to have been entrusted to Privy Councillors only, a comment made in 1855, nicely pinpointed the change of climate. The appearance of the *Edinburgh* or any other quarterly in the 1850s rarely created a sensation, or even a ripple, in political circles. That they had once done so seemed a curious anachronism in 1855. Even Henry Reeve's comparison of his move from *The Times* to the *Edinburgh* in the same year, as an exchange of the House of Commons for a peerage, accorded the *Edinburgh* a political weight and status which was more sentimental than real by the mid-century.

Surveying the periodical scene at the end of the nineteenth century, Mrs Oliphant was drawn to a reflection which must have been shared by many observers of the period:

> It has, indeed, always been a standing mystery to us where the constantly increasing recruits of this noble army find any readers at all, and we have sometimes thought that the real cause of the constant multiplication might be that nobody in the present day feels called upon to read, while everyone attempts to write, and desires to see him or herself in print.[3]

Coming from a prolific contributor to *Blackwood's* and the author of over a hundred works of fiction, the comment is not without unintentional irony. But the nature and extent of the quarterlies' readership, particularly in the early decades, is not easy to discern.

One historian estimated that at their peak the two major quarterlies had a readership of over 100,000, five times their combined circulation.[4] Even if the figure was only double the circulation figures, the origin of those readers is not altogether clear. They included the so-called intelligentsia, almost certainly, the educated upper-middle classes, the professional classes, the upwardly mobile, literate middle classes and some of the lower-middle classes, the group which Bagehot said needed to be taught what to think. The inclusion of the latter group made the quarterly readership less elitist, less of a mandarin group than might have been thought.

I have suggested earlier that Arnold's inference, in 'The Function of Criticism at the Present Time', that English criticism was stultified by its sectarian origins and by implication its sectarian readership, is incorrect, at least as far as the readership of the quarterlies is concerned. Evidence from diaries like Crabb Robinson's and others suggests that readers were rarely committed ideologically to one quarterly only, and that most read across a spectrum of Reviews. John Stuart Mill's point, that even the politically committed *Edinburgh* and *Quarterly* did not necessarily adopt a political line on non-political subjects, is also important, reinforcing as it does the picture of a relatively homogeneous, serious-minded, earnest readership, rather than a group sub-divided into political or religious camps. The quarterly readership in fact testified to the coherence as well as the eclecticism of the nineteenth-century intelligent reading public, as well as to its intellectual energy. It was a reading public, it is important to remember, which did not have a quality newspaper press at its disposal, either weekly or daily.

What perhaps neither Carlyle nor Hazlitt could have foreseen, when commenting on the reviewing scene in the 1820s and 1830s was the longevity of the phenomenon, the fact that Reviews and reviewing were to remain a dominant feature of the culture throughout the nineteenth century and beyond. The sheer resilience of the two original quarterlies gives one pause. Overtaken politically in the 1840s by the newspapers and outstripped in terms of readership by the weeklies and monthlies of the 1850s and 1860s, the *Edinburgh* endured until 1929, and the *Quarterly*, almost unbelievably, until 1967. In 1877 Mark Pattison wrote that 'those venerable old wooden three-deckers, the *Edinburgh Review* and the *Quarterly Review* still put out to sea under the command, I believe, of the Ancient Mariner'.[5] The legacy of 1802 still had a long way to run.

Notes

1. Quoted by Mrs Gordon, *Christopher North, A Memoir of John Wilson*, 2 vols (Edinburgh: Edmonston and Douglas, 1862), II, 284–5; BL Add. MSS. 346248, f. 428.
2. A. C. Fraser Papers, National Library of Scotland, Price to Fraser, 3 November 1854.
3. Mrs. M. O. W. Oliphant and F. R. Oliphant, *The Victorian Age of English Literature*, 2 vols (London, 1892), II, 301.
4. Elie Halevy, according to John Gross, *The Rise and Fall of the Man of Letter* (London: Weidenfeld and Nicolson, 1969), p.2.
5. *Fortnightly Review*, XXII (1877), 663. Quoted by W. E. Houghton, 'Periodical Literature and the Articulate Classes', in *The Victorian Periodical Press: Samplings and Soundings*, ed. J. Shattock and M. Wolff (Leicester: Leicester University Press, 1982), p.17.

APPENDIX:
PIRATED EDITIONS OF THE
EDINBURGH AND *QUARTERLY*
REVIEWS

Among the imprints of American 'editions' of the *Quarterly* are the following:

New York: Ezra Sargeant, Vol. I, (1810), marked 'London printed, re-printed for Ezra Sargeant'.

New York: James Eastburn, executor to E. Sargeant, Vol. VII.

New York: Eastburn, Kirk & Co., Vols. VIII-XI.

New York: Thos. Kirk & Thos. R. Mercein, Vol. XV (1817), marked 'London Printed, reprinted for...'.

Boston: Wells & Lilly, Vol. XX (1821).

Boston: Lilly & Wait (late Wells & Lilly), Vol. XLIII (1830).

Boston: Lilly, Wait, Colman, & Holden, Vol. XLVIII (1833).

New York: Theodore Foster, Vol. LII (1834), marked 'American Edition'.

New York: William Lewer, Vol. LIX (1837), 'American Edition'.

New York: Jemima M. Lewer, Vol. LXII (1838), 'American Edition'.

New York: Jemima M. Mason, (late Lewer) Vol. LXIV (1839).

New York: Walker, Craighead & Co., Vol. LXXI (1843), 'American Edition'.

New York: Leonard Scott & Co., Vol. CXLI (1876), 'American Edition'.

Philadelphia: Leonard Scott Publ. Co., Vol. CLVII (1884), 'London; John Murray' also on title page.

The imprints for the *Edinburgh* include the following names:

New York: Ezra Sargeant, marked 'Edinburgh printed, reprinted for Ezra Sargeant', Vol. XV (1810).

New York: Eastburn, Kirk & Co., marked 'Edinburgh printed and reprinted for Eastburn, Kirk and Co.', Vol. XX (1813).

New York: Thos. Kirk and Thos. R. Mercein, marked 'Edinburgh printed and reprinted for...', Vol. XXVI (1816).

Boston: Wells and Lilly, Vol. XXXII (1820).

Boston: Lilly and Wait, Vol. LII (1831).

Boston: Lilly, Wait, Colman, and Holden, Vol. LV (1832).

New York: Theodore Foster, Vol. LXI (1835).

New York: William Lewer, Vol. LXVI (1838), marked 'American Edition'.

New York: Jemima M. Mason (late Lewer), Vol. LXIX (1839), marked 'American Edition'.

New York: Leonard Scott & Co., Vol. LXXIX (1844), Vol. CXVII (1863), each marked 'American Edition'.

Philadelphia: Leonard Scott Publishing Co., Vol. CXXI (1884). Edinburgh: Adam and Charles Black also on title page.

This information is based on an examination of copies held by Colby College Library, Waterville, Maine. I am grateful to Professor Eileen M. Curran for drawing them to my attention and for giving me the opportunity to consult them.

SELECT BIBLIOGRAPHY

Primary Sources:

Macvey Napier Correspondence, British Library.
Brougham Papers, University College, London.
Correspondence of John Wilson Croker, William L. Clements Library, University of Michigan.
Correspondence of J.W. Croker, British Library.
Holland House Papers, British Library.
Archives of John Murray Publishers, London.
Lockhart Correspondence, National Library of Scotland.
Jeffrey Correspondence, National Library of Scotland.

Secondary Sources:

Arnold, Matthew, 'The Function of Criticism at the Present Time', *Essays in Criticism*, First Series (London: Macmillan, 1865).
Aspinall, Arthur, *Lord Brougham and the Whig Party* (Manchester: Manchester University Press, 1927).
————, *Politics and the Press 1780-1850* (Hassocks: Harvester, 1973. orig. pub. 1949).
————, ed. *Three Early Nineteenth Century Diaries* (London: Williams & Norgate, 1952).

Bagehot, Walter, 'The First Edinburgh Reviewers', *Literary Studies*, I (London: Longman's, Green, 1884).

Barrow, John, *An Auto-biographical Memoir of Sir John Barrow* (London: John Murray, 1847).

Bennett, Scott, 'Catholic Emancipation, the *Quarterly Review* and Britain's Constitutional Revolution', *Victorian Studies*, XII (1969).

Blake, Robert, *Disraeli* (London: Eyre and Spottiswoode, 1966).

Brightfield, Myron F., *John Wilson Croker* (London: Allen & Unwin, 1940).

————, 'Lockhart's Quarterly Contributions', *PMLA*, LIX (1944).

Bromwich, David, *Hazlitt: The Mind of a Critic* (Oxford: Oxford University Press, 1983)

The Life and Times of Henry Lord Brougham by himself, 3 vols (London and Edinburgh: Blackwood, 1871).

Carlyle, Thomas, 'Characteristics', *Essays*, 4 vols (London: Chapman and Hall, 1857).

The Collected Letters of Thomas and Jane Welsh Carlyle, ed. C. R. Sanders and K. J. Fielding, Duke–Edinburgh edition, 12 vols (Durham, NC: Duke University Press, 1977–85).

Clive, John, *Scotch Reviewers: The Edinburgh Review 1802–1815* (London: Faber, 1957).

————, *Thomas Babington Macaulay: The Shaping of the Historian* (London: Secker and Warburg, 1973).

Cockburn, Henry, *The Life of Lord Jeffrey with a Selection from his Correspondence*, 2 vols (Edinburgh: Adam and Charles Black, 1852).

————, *Journal of Henry Cockburn 1831-1854*, 2 vols (Edinburgh: Edmonston and Douglas, 1874).

————, *Memorials of his Time*, ed. Karl F. C. Miller (London: University of Chicago Press, 1974, orig. pub. 1856).

Collini, Stefan, Winch, Donald, and Burrow, John, *That Noble Science of Politics: A Study in Nineteenth-Century Intellectual History* (Cambridge; Cambridge University Press, 1983).

[Copleston, Edward], *Advice to a Young Reviewer with a Specimen of the Art* (Oxford: J. Parker and J.Cooke, 1807).

The Creevey Papers: A Selection from the Correspondence & Diaries of the late Thomas Creevey M.P. ed. Sir Herbert Maxwell, 2 vols (London: John Murray,1903).

Creevey's Life and Times: A Further Selection from the Correspondence of Thomas Creevey 1760-1838, ed. John Gore (London: John Murray, 1934).

The Croker Papers: The Correspondence and Diaries of John Wilson Croker, ed. Louis J. Jennings, 3 vols (London: John Murray, 1884).

Curran, Eileen M., 'The *Foreign Quarterly Review* 1827–1846: A British Interpretation of Modern European Literature', unpublished doctoral thesis, Cornell University, 1958.

Davis, Margaret C., 'Letters of Croker to Lockhart, Vol. I', unpublished MA thesis, Texas Technological University (1949).

Benjamin Disraeli Letters: 1815-1834, ed. J. A. W. Gunn, John Matthews, Donald M. Schurman and M. G. Weibe, 2 vols (Toronto: University of Toronto Press, 1982).

Fetter, Frank W., 'The Authorship of Economic Articles in the *Edinburgh Review* 1802-1847', *Journal of Political Economy*, LXI (1953).

————, 'The Economic Articles in the *Quarterly Review* and their authors, 1809–1852', *Journal of Political Economy*, LXVI (1958).

Fontana, Biancamaria, *Rethinking the Politics of Commercial Society: The Edinburgh Review 1802–32* (Cambridge: Cambridge University Press, 1985).

[Gleig, G. R.], 'Life of Lockhart', *Quarterly Review*, CXVI (October 1864).

Gordon, Mrs, *Christopher North, a Memoir of John Wilson*, 2 vols (Edinburgh: Edmonston and Douglas, 1862).

[Grant, James], *The Great Metropolis* (London: Saunders and Otley, 1837).

Greig, James A., *Francis Jeffrey of the Edinburgh Review* (Edinburgh: Oliver and Boyd, 1948).

Greville, Charles C. F., *The Greville Memoirs: A Journal of the Reigns of Kings George IV, King William IV and Queen Victoria*, ed. Henry Reeve, 8 vols (London: Longmans, 1888).

Gross, John, *The Rise and Fall of the Man of Letters* (London: Weidenfeld and Nicolson, 1969).

Hart, F. R., *Lockhart as Romantic Biographer* (Edinburgh: Edinburgh University Press, 1971).

Hazlitt, William, 'The Periodical Press', *The Complete Works*, Centenary Ed., ed. P.P. Howe, XVI (London: Dent, 1930–4).

Hildyard, M. C., *Lockhart's Literary Criticism* (London, 1931).

Holland, Henry, Lord, *Memoirs of the Whig Party during my Time*, 2 vols (London, 1852–4).

Elizabeth, Lady Holland to her Son 1821-1845, ed. Earl of Ilchester (London: John Murray, 1908).

Houghton, W. E., ed., *The Wellesley Index to Victorian Periodicals*, 4 vols (Toronto: University of Toronto Press, 1966–88).

————, 'Periodical Literature and the Articulate Classes', in Joanne Shattock and Michael Wolff, ed., *The Victorian Periodical Press: Samplings and Soundings* (Leicester: Leicester University Press, 1982).

Jeffrey, Francis, *Contributions to the Edinburgh Review*, 4 vols (London: Longmans, 1844).

Keithley, X. C. 'The Lockhart–Croker Correspondence, Vol. III', unpublished MA thesis, Texas Technological University (1940).

Kern, John D., Schneider, Elizabeth, and Griggs, Irwin, 'Lockhart to Croker on the Quarterly', *PMLA* X (1945).

Koss, Stephen, *The Rise and Fall of the Political Press in Britain*, 2 vols, *The Nineteenth Century, Vol. I* (London: Hamish Hamilton, 1981).

Kriegel, Abraham, *The Holland House Diaries 1831-1840* (London: Routledge, 1977).

Lang, Andrew, *The Life and Letters of John Gibson Lockhart*, 2 vols (London: John C. Nimmo, 1897).

Laughton, J. K., ed., *Memoirs of the Life and Correspondence of Henry Reeve*, 2 vols (London: Longmans, 1898).

Lewis, Quanah, 'The Lockhart-Croker Correspondence, Vol. II', unpublished MA thesis, Texas Technological University, (1940).

Lively, Jack, and Rees, John, eds, *Utilitarian Logic and Politics: James Mill's 'Essay on Government', Macaulay's Critique and the Ensuing Debate* (Oxford: Oxford University Press, 1978).

Lloyd, Christopher, *Mr. Barrow of the Admiralty: A Life of Sir John Barrow 1764-1848* (London: Collins, 1970).

Lockhart, John Gibson, *Memoirs of the Life of Scott*, 7 vols (Edinburgh: Robert Cadell, 1837–8).

————, *Peter's Letters to his Kinfolk*, ed. William Ruddick (Edinburgh: Scottish Academic Press, 1977).

Lockhead, Marion, *John Gibson Lockhart* (London: John Murray, 1954).

Lott, Woodrow Wilson, 'The Lockhart–Croker Correspondence, Vol. I', unpublished MA thesis, Texas Technological University, (1940).

Martineau, Harriet, *Biographical Sketches 1852-1868* (London: Macmillan, 1870).

Harriet Martineau's Autobiography with memorials by M. W. Chapman, 3 vols (London: Smith, Elder, 1877).

The Letters of Thomas Babington Macaulay, ed. Thomas Pinney, 6 vols (Cambridge: Cambridge University Press, 1974).

Maurer, Oscar, 'Anonymity vs. Signature in Victorian Reviewing', *University of Texas Studies in English*, XXVII (1948).

Mill, James and Mill, John Stuart, 'Periodical Literature. Edinburgh Review', *Westminster Review*, I (January, April 1824).

Mill, John Stuart, *Autobiography and Literary Essays*, ed. J. M. Robson and Jack Stillinger, *The Collected Works of J. S. Mill* Vol. I (London: Routledge, 1981).

The Earlier Letters of John Stuart Mill, ed. Francis E. Mineka, 2 vols, *The Collected Works of John Stuart Mill 1812-1848*, XII, XIII (London: Routledge, 1963).

The Later Letters of John Stuart Mill 1849-1873, ed. Francis E. Mineka and D.N. Lindley, 4 vols, *The Collected Works of John Stuart Mill*, XIV-XVII (London: Routledge, 1972).

Millgate, Jane, 'Father and Son: Macaulay's *Edinburgh* Debut', *Review of English Studies*, N.S.21 (1970).

Millgate, Jane, *Macaulay*, Routledge Author Guides (London: Routledge and Kegan Paul, 1973).

Milne, J. Maurice, 'The Politics of *Blackwood's* 1817–1846: A study of the political, economic and social articles in *Blackwood's Edinburgh Magazine* and of selected contributors', unpublished doctoral thesis, Newcastle University, 1984.

Mitchell, Austin Vernon, *The Whigs in Opposition 1815–1830* (Oxford: Clarendon Press, 1967).

Monypenny, W. F. and Buckle, G. E., *The Life of Disraeli*, 2 vols rev. ed. (London: John Murray, 1929).

Morgan, Peter F., *Literary Critics and Reviewers in Early 19th Century Britain* (London: Croom Helm, 1983).

Morley, John, 'Memorials of a Man of Letters', in *Nineteenth Century Essays*, ed. Peter Stansky (London: University of Chicago Press, 1970).

Selection from the Correspondence of the late Macvey Napier, ed. by his son (London: Macmillan, 1879).

Nesbitt, George L., *Benthamite Reviewing: The First Twelve Years of the Westminster Review 1824–1836* (New York: Columbia University Press, 1934).

New, Chester, *The Life of Henry Brougham to 1830* (Oxford: Clarendon Press, 1961).

Nickerson, Charles C., 'Disraeli, Lockhart and Murray: an Episode in the History of the *Quarterly Review*', *Victorian Studies*, XV (1972).

Paston, George, *At John Murray's: Records of a Literary Circle 1843-1892* (London: John Murray, 1932).

'The Centenary of the Quarterly Review', *Quarterly Review*, CCX-CCXI (1909).

Reeves, Emma B., 'Letters of Croker to Lockhart Vol. II', unpublished MA thesis, Texas Technological University (1949).

Diary, Reminiscences and Correspondence of Henry Crabb Robinson, ed. Thomas Sadler, 3 vols (London: Macmillan, 1869).

Henry Crabb Robinson on Books and their Writers, ed. Edith J. Morley, 3 vols (London: Dent, 1938).

Roebuck, J. A., *History of the Whig Ministry of 1830*, 2 vols (London, 1852).

Roper, Derek, *Reviewing before the Edinburgh 1788–1802* (Newark, N J: University of Delaware Press, 1978).

Rosenberg, Sheila, 'The Financing of Radical Opinion: John Chapman and the Westminster Review', in Joanne Shattock and Michael Wolff, ed. *The Victorian Periodical Press: Samplings and Soundings* (Leicester: Leicester University Press, 1982).

Sanders, L.C., ed., *The Holland House Circle* (London: Methuen, 1908).

The Letters of Sir Walter Scott, ed. H. J. C. Grierson, 12 vols, Centenary Edition (London: Constable, 1932).

The Familiar Letters of Sir Walter Scott, 2 vols (Edinburgh: David Douglas, 1894).

The Private Letter-Books of Sir Walter Scott, ed. Wilfred Partington (London: Hodder and Stoughton, 1930).

The Journal of Sir Walter Scott, 2 vols (Edinburgh: David Douglas, 1890).

Shannon, Edgar F., *Tennyson and the Reviewers* (Cambridge, Mass.: Harvard University Press, 1952, repr. 1967).

Shattock, Joanne, 'Spreading it Thinly; some Victorian Reviewers at Work', *Victorian Periodicals Newsletter*, IX (September 1976).

Shattock, Joanne and Wolff, Michael, ed, *The Victorian Periodical Press: Samplings and Soundings* (Leicester: Leicester University Press, 1982).

Shine, Hill and Shine, Helen, *The Quarterly Review under Gifford 1809-1824* (Chapel Hill, NC: University of North Carolina Press, 1949).

Smiles, Samuel, *A Publisher and his Friends. Memoir of John Murray*, 2 vols (London: John Murray, 1891).

Smith, Simon Nowell, ed., *Selected Letters of Sydney Smith* (Oxford:

Oxford University Press, 1953).

Southey, C.C., *The Life and Correspondence of the late Robert Southey*, 6 vols (London: Longman, 1849–50).

Selections from the Letters of Southey, ed. J. W. Warter, 4 vols (London, 1856)

New Letters of Southey, ed. K. Curry, 2 vols (New York: Columbia University Press, 1965)

Southgate, Donald, *The Passing of the Whigs 1832–1886* (London: Macmillan, 1962).

Stang, Robert, *The Theory of the Novel in England 1850–1870* (London: Routledge, 1961).

Stephen, Leslie, 'The First Edinburgh Reviewers', *Hours in a Library*, II (London: Smith, Elder, 1899).

Stewart, Robert, *Henry Brougham 1778–1868: His Public Career* (London: Bodley Head, 1985).

Strangways, Giles Stephen Holland Fox, Earl of Ilchester, *Chronicles of Holland House 1820–1900* (London: John Murray, 1937).

Strout, A. L. ed., 'Some Unpublished Letters of John Gibson Lockhart to John Wilson Croker', *Notes and Queries*, CLXXV, CLXXXV–CLXXXIX, 22, 29 October 1938; 11, 25 September, 9 October 1943; 9, 23 September, 7, 21 October, 4, 18 November 1944; 2, 30 June, 14, 28 July, 11, 25 August, 8, 22 September, 6, 20 October, 3 November 1945; 9, 23 March, 20 April, 4, 18 May, 1, 15 June 1946.

Tener, Robert H., 'Breaking the Code of Anonymity: The Case of the *Spectator* 1861–1897', *Yearbook of English Studies*, XVI (1986).

Tillotson, Kathleen, *Novels of the Eighteen Forties* (Oxford: Clarendon Press, 1959).

Trevelyan. G. O., *Life and Letters of Lord Macaulay*, 2 vols (London: Longmans, 1876).

Despatches, Correspondence and Memoranda of Field Marshall Arthur Duke of Wellington, 8 vols (London: John Murray, 1867-80).

Wiley, Nell M., 'The Lockhart–Croker Correspondence, Vol. IV', unpublished MA thesis, Texas Technological University (1940).

Wilson, David A., *Life of Thomas Carlyle*, 6 vols, *Carlyle to 'The French Revolution'*, vol. 2 (London: Kegan, Paul, 1926-37).

Young, William, *The History of Dulwich College*, 2 vols (London: T. B. Bumpus, 1889).

INDEX

Note: the abbreviations *ER* and *QR* refer to the *Edinburgh Review* and the *Quarterly Review*

DATE DUE

MAR 2 5 1997			
APR 11 1997			
			Printed in USA